THE KITTEN
WHISPERER

THE KITTEN
WHISPERER

A LEADING CAT EXPERT EXPLAINS THE SECRETS
OF HOW TO GIVE YOUR CAT THE
BEST POSSIBLE START IN LIFE

CLAIRE
BESSANT

BARRON'S

First edition for the United States, its territories and dependencies,
and the Philippine Republic published in 2005 by Barron's
Educational Series, Inc.

First published in hardback in 2004 by
Metro Publishing Ltd
3 Bramber Court
2 Bramber Road
London W14 9PB, England

All inquiries should be addressed to:
Barron's Educational Series, Inc.
250 Wireless Boulevard
Hauppauge, New York 11788
www.barronseduc.com

International Standard Book No. 0-7641-3053-6

Library of Congress Catalog Card No. 2004104619

Printed in China

9 8 7 6 5 4 3 2 1

Contents

Introduction

A kitten is one of nature's very pretty things – small and vulnerable, fluffy and wide-eyed. It has the potential to be a wild animal or to enjoy a life closely intertwined with yours or mine. Just how a kitten begins its life can make the difference between how closely it is suited to one of these options and how much it enjoys the life ahead of it.

While some things are, no matter what we do, pre-set in feline behavior, we can still make a large impact on how closely and happily our cats live alongside us. People who breed cats, either on purpose or, as often happens with moggies (mixed breeds), by accident, have a large responsibility for how their kittens develop both in terms of confidence and ability to interact with people and everything associated with human lifestyles. By choosing the right kitten and understanding its development and its needs, we can try to nurture one of these small creatures into a confident, loving, and lovable adult cat which we can enjoy sharing our lives with for fourteen or more years.

Aim for Perfection

OK – there is no such thing as the perfect kitten, just as there is no such thing as the perfect child. However, you would have to admit that kittens have perfect looks and if they didn't have to interact with us, they would probably have behavior perfect for the job at hand – surviving. Living with humans does somewhat muddy the waters, though, because we want to have a relationship with our cats and to have them live closely with us (mostly on our terms). We can inadvertently come between a cat and its natural behaviors – this is where the whispering comes in!

When you think about it, a relationship between mankind and cats is a somewhat strange one. On the other hand, the human/canine relationship seems a bit more natural; both species are very sociable and have evolved complex signals and ways of living with their own kind that involve give and take, compromise, and a structure that helps them to maintain the success. These structures can work quite well between the two species when they live together since humans and canines both work from a similar rule book.

Cats, on the other hand, have evolved from a species known for solitary living (except when females have kittens). Our domestic cats do live in groups in a farm or feral situation (i.e., when they live wild and have had little or no contact with people). These groups have some structure and purpose, but not in such a complex sense as would be the case with dogs. Cats can live in groups where resources such as food and shelter are bountiful (for example, in a farmyard) but will revert to being alone if the resources available will support only one cat. The cat is an obligatory carnivore – it has to eat meat in order to survive and therefore is specialized in its hunting. It does not cooperate to hunt. Thus the parallel with human society is not a strong one. If you stand back and try to look on it with a fresh perspective, you can understand why it would seem strange to someone from another world that we live so closely with this very different species. However, we know the relationship can and does work very well and that both cats and humans benefit greatly from it. What we need to know is whether there are things that will make it difficult to keep both parties happy or if there are aspects of how we live together that can make the bond stronger. What we can aim for is giving the relationship we have with our cats the best possible chance. We can try to influence or control as many of the variables as possible in order to avoid the obvious pitfalls. We can have a stab at choosing a cat with a personality that is adaptable to our lifestyle and work to bond with our cats.

Some cat owners who have had a long, happy, and very satisfying relationship with their cats may wonder what all the fuss is for. Others will be only too aware of what I am talking about. There are some pitfalls for the unwary or the unlucky that can lead to a poor relationship – perhaps a kitten (and subsequently a cat) that has hidden under the couch for the past six years, or one that is aggressive with the children and can be very difficult to live with. Luckily, the cat is a very adaptable creature, and most of us have managed to cope well. We have been lucky in taking on a cat without really knowing what we are doing, and have ended up with a pet that we are content to live with.

What can we do, then, to minimize the possibilities of getting it wrong? How do you choose your perfect kitten? First of all, it comes down to doing some homework – research really does pay off.

People who have read some of my other books will know what is coming next, and I will be brief this time. Forget all your views on cats – pretend this is a creature you have not come across before and get to know it a little from a natural history point of view. We should be looking at our cats from a position of respect – even awe! Here is a creature that is equipped with some top-of-the-line sensors, a body that is designed for power, stealth, flexibility, accuracy, and the ability to kill. And, while many of the skills it has are inherent, many also have to be learned. A cat has to be a very fast learner – in the wild a female cat may have two or three litters a year. The kittens will have to go from being small, vulnerable, blind, and fairly immobile newborns to agile, independent creatures that can hunt and kill other small animals with all of the skills which that entails – and all in about four months. By that time their mother will already have another litter to care for or one on the way imminently. We may look at our well-fed pet cats that seem to have the life of Riley, lounging on the windowsill, and think that cats don't have a bad or stressful life. However, given a twist of fate that results in a cat being born a feral kitten rather than a pet, the ability to learn fast makes all the difference between life and death. All that play might look fun but it has very serious implications. Even the fluffy Persian curled up on the couch has these instincts built in, although it might be better at hiding them than some breeds or individuals.

Perhaps what I am saying is that we shouldn't take cats for granted and assume they are simply there as companions that look very lovely and purr on our laps; we shouldn't get upset if they decide to catch a bird or don't come to us when we want them. There is a very thin line between domestication and the wild where cats are concerned. Indeed, a cat that has started out as a pet can revert to living wild if it wants or needs to, and then go back to being a pet again if the opportunity arises. It is, however, much more difficult to go the other way, as we will find out later.

So step back – look at how cats interact with the world without us, read up on how they see and feel the world, and look at their graceful movements, their amazing weapons and how skillfully they use them if they need to, and say wow! Respect is always a good starting point from whence to indulge in the feline species. You will get much more from your cat, you will look at it differently, and you will understand it much more if you know what it was really meant for – not just being a purring hot-water bottle! And knowing more about your cat will also help you to sort out problems when things go wrong. Don't assume or expect your cat to do certain things but be delighted if it does. Lecture over!

When we look for human partners, we think we know what we are looking for, the personality we like, and the kind of relationship we expect. Of course, even with our own kind we often get it all wrong and here we are speaking the same language and supposedly working from the same rule book. (There are many men from Mars and women from Venus who may disagree with this!) You may not think you have any preconceptions about how you want your cat to be, but examine the pictures in your mind. You may expect it to be like a cat you have had before, like the cat of a friend, or one you have seen on television. Perhaps you have not really even thought about it consciously, but you still have an ideal image in your mind.

One thing that scientists and owners agree on is that cats all have very individual personalities – every one is different. There will be a broad range of these personalities that will fit into your lifestyle and what you want from your cat – the more flexible you are, the less difficult it is, and the more adaptable the cat, the easier it is as well. Chapter 2 will look at what we want from our cats – how flexible are you about what you expect or accept or what your family or lifestyle can deal with? Chapter 3 will look at what shapes a cat's personality and behavior, and what conditions make a cat more flexible or adaptable in its approach to us. There are things we can do to help improve the chances of a successful partnership. Your homework is to examine what you want from your cat in terms of behavior toward you and, if you have one, your family; the conditions you want it to be happy living in; how much attention you want to give to or get from your cat; whether you want it to be sociable with your friends; or if it would be happy with a quiet, secret companion nobody else sees. There are cats to fit all of these requirements – I hope this book will help you look in the right places to find the one that suits you.

The more you find out about cat behavior, the more you realize that much of what shapes how a cat interacts with the world is actually outside the influence of its owner unless he or she actually breeds the litter. The largest influences on a kitten's development are of course genetics – what we often term nature (its genetic inheritance) – and nurture (how it is cared for) in the first two months of life. Cats' personalities do change as they get older but few undergo drastic change without drastic cause. Most will gradually get wilder or tamer, more tolerant or less tolerant, more demanding or less so, depending on a combination of their early experiences as well as their owner's care for them. There can be changes and the relationship can be brought closer or broken altogether by our own behavior with and to our cats, so it is worth working to build the relationship. However, understanding how personality is formed should make us shy of expecting miracles. There are always tales of people who say they have tamed the fiercest feral or brought around the most nervous of cats. These are not the norm, though; they may be extraordinary cases following extraordinary care but they are not that common. For busy people who do not have lots of time to spend with and on their cat, it is easier to avoid these extremes than to try and solve the problem. This will be explored further in Chapter 2.

Finally, the health of your cat can have a large bearing on how happily it lives with you. Health affects well-being, confidence, and energy. Cats have nobody to rely on but themselves; if they feel unwell then they will be even more careful not to take risks or put themselves in a situation that they feel is threatening. There are many motives for taking on a sickly kitten, but bear in mind that its illness may be long term, making it very difficult to assess how the kitten might behave when healthy. Some people will be happy to risk this; others will not.

The next few chapters aim to make you think about the kitten you are taking on – whether you actually want a kitten, what you want from it, what may influence its personality, and how you can try to balance these factors to try and get your perfect kitten. It will become your perfect cat perhaps for the next fourteen years or so – in other words, it's worth your time and effort.

The Making of a Kitten – the Foundation of a Cat

The range of personalities and behaviors cats exhibit in association with people can vary from the very fearful cat that lives its life mostly hiding under the bed to the overattached cat that starts to mutilate itself because its owners have gone out and left it alone for the day. Any cat, despite its parentage (pedigree or moggie), can exhibit either of these behaviors and lots of variations in between. So what might make a seemingly independent moggie become a cat unable to function without its owner present or turn a seemingly well-bred pedigree cat into a frightened fugitive? People who have worked with cats, in particular feral cats, have found that these extremes can be the result of a kitten's experiences within a very short period of time early in its life – what is called the sensitive period for socialization. This would seem to support the argument that nurture rather than nature is all important. However, it is not quite as simple as that – as I will explain later on.

INHERITANCE

To what extent do we inherit our personality (what we term "nature") and to what extent are we a product of our environment and our early experiences (what we term "nurture")? This is hard enough to answer in relation to people, who can voice their inner thoughts, so it may be an extremely difficult problem to untangle in felines. However, work that has been carried out in a variety of areas related to this question can give us some clues.

Researchers have identified that cats have different personality types. They have categorized some felines as being sociable, confident, easy-going, trusting, interactive, bold, and likely to initiate friendly interactions. They have classed others as timid or shy, unfriendly or nervous.

Owners will recognize which of their own cats fall into these categories. Is it genes or experiences that make them turn out this way? Let's look at what we know.

PARENTS

Research has revealed that kittens with friendly, outgoing fathers are more likely to be inquisitive and confident – daring to explore strange people and new things in their environment. Likewise, a friendly mother is likely to pass on a disposition for confidence in her kittens. With mothers there is much more than simply genetics to consider – unlike the father's contribution, which is almost always simply limited to providing genetic material! At the end of this chapter we look at the importance of the mother cat's attitude to life and how this affects the kittens. We will start to understand the complex interactions between genetics and what we call nurture – the kitten's upbringing and exposure to the world around it.

Another aspect that may have a strong impact on the kitten's behavior is again dependent on its parents – its breed. Breeding pedigree cats means that the parents are chosen from a limited gene pool (certain members of that breed) for mating. As the breed is developed for certain looks, it may also develop certain behavioral characteristics. For example, the Siamese breed is known to be very vocal, while the Persian is much quieter. That is not to say you cannot have a very noisy Persian and a very quiet Siamese – it has been found that individual characters of cats range more broadly than breed characteristics. However, some breeds do have a greater tendency to behave in certain ways.

A survey on cat personalities published by the U.K.'s Feline Advisory Bureau in 2004 found that the owners of pedigree cats rated their cats as more confident than owners of moggies did. The owners who completed the questionnaire were asked forty questions about their cats' backgrounds and current behavior, such as how they played, how noisy they were, whether they were territorial, and whether they liked dogs or people – or even catnip!

The survey looked at over 1,800 cats; about 720 of these were pedigrees and the rest were moggies. One of the survey's findings was that moggies were twice as likely to be nervous of new people and things as pedigree cats were. Some of the least nervous breeds were Norwegian Forest Cats, Ragdolls, Burmese, and Tonkinese. This is an interesting finding but it must be looked at in context. One-third of moggies in the survey came from shelters – for many their background was unknown and thus their level of socialization during that critical period was also questionable. It was an excellent finding for pedigrees and suggests that breeders are taking the time and effort to socialize their kittens and to choose not just for looks but also for temperament.

What about color?

Does color influence personality in any way? We think of human redheads and chestnut horses as a bit fiery and unpredictable. Is there a feline equivalent? Strangely enough, tortoiseshell cats do have a reputation for being less than tolerant of cats or people they do not approve of and are considered rather feisty. In the personality survey carried out by the Feline Advisory Bureau there was no evidence of this but the survey did show that, in moggies, tabbies and gingers were more bold than black-and-white cats. There was not a major difference but it was an interesting result.

Sex

Of course, the sex of a cat does have an influence on its behavior and is one of the inherited characteristics that will guarantee certain behaviors such as calling in sexually mature females and the various territorial and confrontational behaviors associated with intact males. However, unless you intend to breed your cat (and that requires very considerable thought) you will be neutering it. From the point of view of behavior, neutering does indeed neutralize the extremes of behavior. (We will have another quick look at whether getting a male or female kitten is right for you in Chapter 4.)

KITTEN DEVELOPMENT

Before looking at the so-called sensitive period of social development that affects how cats interact with the world of people, other animals, and other cats, it is useful to plot the development of kittens from birth. Realizing how they are learning and dealing with the world around them through use of their rapidly developing, exceptional senses can give us an idea of the huge volume of information, behaviors, and body control that kittens must develop in a very short period of time.

When a kitten is born, it has poorly developed hearing (the ears are covered by folds of skin) and its eyes are closed. It will raise its head in reaction to loud noises, so perhaps its world is quite muffled at this point; with no sight and poor hearing, its senses are focused on sensations of touch and smell. Driven by hunger and a desire to stay warm and to be near its mother, the kitten locates the teat through a combination of warmth, touch, and smell. It is thought that the kitten follows a trail of saliva laid down by the mother after birth that leads to the nipples.

Warmth is very important since the kitten cannot yet regulate its own body temperature and has very little control over its limbs or body movements. It will cry if it becomes separated from its mother and will drag itself back toward the litter with short rowing or paddling movements if it gets pushed away by the other kittens.

Once at the teats the kitten latches on to a nipple using bobbing movements of the head, known as the rooting reflex. We see the same thing in our own babies, and like humans the kitten has a sucking reflex that causes it to turn its head toward any object, such as a finger, that touches the area around its mouth. This will gradually be lost as the kitten gets to know where the teat is and how to latch on successfully. The kitten will also make treading movements around the teats to stimulate the flow of milk – this kneading behavior is often seen in adult cats when they sit on our laps and open and close their paws and claws as if in bliss. This is then combined with the purr – a signal to the mother that all is OK and to the others that food has arrived. The mother will also purr as she enters the nest, perhaps a quiet sign that she is back and all is safe. The sound does not carry far, and it can be made while the kittens are sucking so no attention is drawn to the nest. The kitten may suck for as long as eight hours a day and double its weight from about 3.5 to 7 ounces (100 to 200 g) in the first week.

The mother (sometimes referred to as the "queen") may decide to move her kittens after a few days to a new nest, perhaps because the nest is soiled after the birth (even though she will have cleaned up all the placentas) or just because she feels somewhere else may be safer or better suited to the growth and development of the kittens. She will carry each kitten individually by the scruff of the neck. Being picked up in this way causes the kitten to react automatically in a certain way – its front legs become limp and its back legs and tail curl up and out of the way. Presumably if they simply hung down limply, they might catch on the ground or get stepped on by the queen as she negotiates the removal of the kittens to a new den. The kitten will not struggle or make any noise and almost seems immobilized. This reflex continues into adulthood in many cats and can be useful for restraint in an emergency.

By the end of the first week, the kitten is starting to crawl; by about seventeen days, it will start to stand up, albeit in a rather wobbly fashion. The milk teeth start to come through at around two weeks of age and the eyes open after about ten days, although this can vary from two to around sixteen days. Although the eyes are open, the kitten will not be seeing with razor-sharp vision. During this period the eye and the brain are working together to understand what the kitten is seeing and to make sense of the world around it. By four weeks the kitten is able to assess depth and judge distance accurately and will follow moving objects by sight alone; the development of sight will continue until sixteen weeks. The ears are also functional by about two weeks old and fully developed by four weeks.

In its first three weeks of life the kitten will rely entirely on its mother for nutrition. However, in the third week the kitten may spend a minute or two every day trying out solid food. It will watch its mother and try what she is eating – indeed, this may have a strong influence on what it likes to eat later in life.

Until this point the queen has made sure that all the kittens were offered milk and encouraged to feed. From three weeks she will start to stay away from the litter a little longer, and when she returns she will lie in such a way that her teats are inaccessible. The kittens are growing fast and in the wild would be depleting her reserves considerably as she would not have had the time to hunt and catch enough to feed all of the kittens via her milk. Initially the kittens will try harder to access the milk, but at the same time she will distract them with solid food or prey. This redirection of their attention and energy is a very important part of growing up, as they learn to deal with frustration and the conflict they feel on no longer being allowed free access to milk. It must come as quite a shock to them initially. Coping with frustration through weaning is one of the first of many challenges that a kitten will face in its life. It is not always possible for a living thing to have exactly what it wants whenever it wants it, and learning this early on encourages cats to be adaptable and able to compromise – and, ultimately, to fit into family life more easily.

Interestingly, up to the point of weaning, the kittens have played a great deal with each other – in what is called social play. However, they now switch more to playing with objects, which is perhaps the next step in preparation for hunting skills. While hunting itself seems to be instinctive, how good they are at it requires practice, and a good teacher (the mother) will help too.

Between three and four weeks old the kitten will gain self-control over urination and defecation, which previously only occurred at the initiation of the mother stimulating the area under the tail. When the mother was in control, she ate the waste so that the nest was not soiled. Now the kittens learn to move away from the nest to urinate and defecate and will also start to paw at litter in the litter box – again, watching the mother is a great stimulus for this behavior. Amazingly, the kitten will be moving confidently by four weeks of age and will be running and enjoying the beginnings of its excellent balance by five weeks. This physical coordination will not be perfected for another five or six weeks but is already quite impressive.

Another very important feline behavior starts at around five weeks – the kitten will groom itself and its littermates. Grooming will keep the coat healthy and clean but seems to have several other functions. First of all, it is part of the kitten's social contact with its mother and its littermates. Grooming also seems to have a calming and comforting influence and gives pleasure – which is perhaps why most cats enjoy being stroked.

The time from about two to seven or eight weeks of age is known as the sensitive period for socialization in humans and other animals. During this period, a young kitten forms relationships with members of its own species and learns how to deal with other species. It is a period you will find referred to again and again in this book and is the make-or-break stage that can determine how the animal deals with life as a pet.

During this socialization period, the kitten learns how to respond to other kittens and, like any growing child, will spend more time with them and less with its mother. Kitten play can be very wild and exuberant and sometimes rather rough. The kittens learn to inhibit themselves and keep their claws sheathed, practicing avoidance rather than simply going for out-and-out war!

The socialization phase lasts up to about fourteen weeks of age (although the sensitive period for learning about people and other species only lasts until about eight weeks old). By this time most kittens have already gone to their new homes. If they are pedigree cats, they will just be moving to their new owners. We will look at further development and how these phases can relate to human growth in Chapter 12.

TIMING IS IMPORTANT

There has been much discussion of the nature-versus-nurture argument over recent years, and of what effects our genes and our environmental experiences have on our characters. As with everything, the extremes of both sides of the argument very seldom offer a complete answer. We live in an age where scientists have started to look at our genomes and those of the animals around us and study what happens in our brains as we develop. Although we are probably still missing a great deal of what is going on, it is becoming clear that, in fact, our genes can be switched on and off by certain things in our experience or environment. Hence, our future is not set in stone when we are born – there is not a map for our lives and how we will live them, how we will react or develop. Rather, there are potential reactions that may or may not be switched on depending on our experiences. Experiences influence genes and genes may dictate how influenced we are by our experiences – a complex interaction that allows for a very wide range of final personalities and behaviors.

But it is not as simple as that! We are learning that there are certain critical or sensitive periods – times during which the wet cement of character can be set in different ways – but that some of these have a finite limit as to how wet the cement is. Once it is set, there may be little we can do to change those pathways of behavior.

Take, for example, extreme cases such as the behavior of geese, which bond to or imprint the first thing they see and follow this as their mother. When a chick imprints on its mother, memories are laid down and a series of changes occur on the left side of the brain that accompany imprinting – neurons alter shape, synapses (junctions between nerve fibers) form, and genes are switched on. If this part of the brain is damaged, the chick does not imprint on its mother. A neurotransmitter is also switched on but the receptor for this transmitter is switched off about ten hours later. Hence there is a limited time known as the critical period when changes to this part of the brain can occur and allow the chick to imprint on its mother.

Other research has found that children who have not had good vision early in their lives but have treatment to correct the physical problem in the eye later on never really learn to see as strong-sighted people do – they have not learned how to interpret what they see; it is too late. If the brain is not taught and programmed by experiences, it cannot interpret what the eyes see – the critical period has passed. Scientists have also found that in monkeys the brain is able to change as it develops during a certain period after birth – it can be shaped by experience – but then loses the ability to be so adaptable. Experience seems to switch on certain genes for the learning process of seeing.

Another example of a critical period is the taking on of an accent. The ability to absorb and change is easy for the young, but inflexibility sets in later on in life. Even if people have lived for fifty years of their adult life in a certain country, they may still maintain the accent of the country where they spent their first fifteen to twenty-five years. Indeed, the ability to learn language, with all of its grammatical complexities, may end at around puberty in humans. This has been demonstrated by several cases of feral children who had been kept alone or grown up on their own in the wild and had not been spoken to for up to the first thirteen years of their lives. They were not able to learn grammar or how to manipulate language even though they did learn a reasonable vocabulary. One of these children was found to be highly intelligent but never learned to speak. If the brain does not become trained by listening and responding to language, it does not develop. There seems to be a period after which it is simply too late for the brain to be able to make the correct pathways.

We use the term "critical" when there is some sort of genetic switch that limits the time during which learning can occur. While the first eight weeks of a cat's life may not quite be critical to its learning to accept other species, this period is vitally important. If this sensitive time is missed, the cat can experience many problems in adapting to life with people.

During this sensitive period, a cat can learn to accept people, other cats, and other animals. Cats are also very adaptable to learning from new experiences during this time (a process known as habituation) as their bodies are not yet reacting to certain events with fear. This gives a kitten time to learn how to react and respond to different situations rather than being flooded by responses that urge it to run away. At seven or eight weeks old the kitten's body primes itself to become much more reactive. Hence the cat has a limited period in which to process its brain to learn how it will deal with these kinds of experiences in the future. It is a time when the cat most readily picks up social behavior. For pet cats this means the socialization of kittens to other cats, humans, and other pets that the kitten is likely to have to live with as it grows and becomes an adult. It is also a time when the kitten learns how to deal with new objects and experiences in a confident manner – getting used to dealing with novel sights, sounds, feelings, and experiences.

In cats the critical sensitive period for socialization seems to be between around two and seven weeks of age. Thereafter, no matter how good the care and socialization, it is very hard to ever forge those pathways that will lead to a cat that is relaxed and happy around people and in its immediate environment, with the usual occurrences such as household noise and movements. This is very important, especially for breeders. Breeders need to ensure that their kittens have regular handling, which has been shown to speed up various physical and behavioral traits and generally to reduce fearfulness. It is important that kittens meet more than one person – encounters with at least four people will help them to be relaxed with humans in general instead of just one or two selected people. In turn, the people also need to spend time with kittens – kittens handled for forty minutes a day have been found to be more attached to people than those handled for fifteen minutes a day. However, you don't have to overdo it – spending longer than forty minutes with a kitten did not result in the same increase in benefit. Of course, it won't do any harm but, if your time is limited, aim for a minimum of about three-quarters of an hour.

THE IMPORTANCE OF MOTHER

As far back as 1930, scientists working with monkeys found that young monkeys taken from their mother to be reared in isolated conditions that were deliberately kept very clean so that they could be free of disease grew up into fearful, antisocial, and seemingly very unhappy adults.

Other related work studied the offspring of highly strung monkeys that were raised by adoptive mothers for their first six months of life. A genetically nervous baby reared by a genetically nervous foster-mother turned out to be a socially incompetent adult, vulnerable to stress, and itself a bad parent. Other monkeys with the same highly strung genetic mothers raised by calm foster-mothers became quite normal, were sociable with other monkeys, and did not become stressed. Thus, in spite of having the genes for a nervous disposition, monkeys could become calm and sociable and even bring up their own babies well if raised by a calm and unstressed mother. It would seem that the ability to mother is learned rather than inherited. The studies also revealed that some monkeys were genetically programmed to be almost unaffected by maternal deprivation while others had a very strong and long-lasting reaction to it. Again, this is evidence of genes working with nature to produce individuals that deal differently with the challenges of everyday living.

Likewise, scientists who have worked with cats have found that the queen, as the first cat with which the kittens have social interactions, is critical to their ability to learn social behavior. Kittens rely on their mother to show them how to respond and interact with events and other beings around them. If their mother is calm and relaxed when people are around during that sensitive socialization period mentioned above, they socialize much better with people. If she is absent, they do not socialize so readily.

Another factor is the health of the kittens and their mother. A queen who is very stressed because she does not have enough food to feed herself to provide milk for her kittens may be reactive and nervous. In humans, mothers suffering from postnatal depression who do not want to interact with their babies in what healthy mothers would call a normal way do actually affect the development of the children – sometimes just temporarily, sometimes for a long time. It has been found that undernourished queens are more aggressive to their kittens and this can affect not only the kittens themselves but also the way they behave with their own offspring. Kittens born of a severely malnourished mother may well have poorer learning aptitude, show less tolerance toward other cats, and have higher levels of reactivity (such as the tendency to run away or to show aggression) if they find themselves in a stressful situation in which they cannot cope. Likewise, unhealthy kittens will lag behind in their physical and behavioral development. And when kittens are growing up and learning, there is not much time for hanging around waiting for others to catch up. A slowing down of physical development may also mean a slowdown in brain development.

The best socialization of kittens, and hence cats, occurs when the mother is healthy and well fed and reacts to people in a relaxed and happy manner. It also helps if she is present when the kittens are getting used to people and shows them that all is well.

Kittens learn lots by watching – they have a great deal to assimilate in a very short period of time. Compare what a cat has to learn with, say, a deer. A deer must be able to run from just about the time it is born and its food is all around. While it needs to learn about predators and fitting in with the herd, its skill base is not exceptional. A kitten starts from a position that is much less developed physically – it certainly can't get up and run away. In two to three months it has to go from being a small, helpless creature to one capable of finding, stalking, catching, and killing its every meal (those unlucky enough not to have owners who feed them, anyway). The skills required to do this are exceptional – the various sensory systems have to go from virtually zero to high quality or the kitten may not survive. Some of the systems and behaviors the kitten exhibits will be automatic; others need a great deal of use to coordinate all of the animal's exceptional senses. As discussed earlier, the brain has to work with the eye to understand what the kitten is seeing; it has to recognize what is happening and then learn to act appropriately. The cat has an amazing sense of balance, which also no doubt takes a great deal of work to get used to and use to best effect. I can imagine it is a bit like learning to drive a Maserati instead of a compact. You have a few short weeks not only to learn to drive but to be able to do stunts too! No wonder kittens excel at learning by watching. They need to watch, understand, and then practice maneuvers. Researchers have found that kittens learn something new more quickly if they see an adult cat performing the task first. How else would they learn the intricate skills of hunting?

While some hunting activities, such as jumping on prey, seem to be preprogrammed, automatic responses to movement, a mother cat will step in and teach the kitten how to perfect the skill and kill the prey if it has not managed to figure it out for itself.

Humans sometimes take over the role of mother cat if the real mother, for whatever reason, cannot look after her own kittens. Hand-rearing is not to be undertaken lightly. It is very hard work, as tiny kittens have to be fed every couple of hours (they need ten feedings a day in the first two weeks, seven a day for the next two weeks, and five a day until they are five weeks old). Kittens that do not get their mother's colostrum (the thin, milky secretion from the nipples that precedes and follows true lactation) may have weakened immunity and will be prone to infection – they can die very easily.

One might imagine that hand-reared kittens would be very people-friendly given what has been discussed about the need for handling at an early age. Surely such well-handled kittens would be closely bonded to their human mothers? In fact, many owners of hand-reared kittens have found that, as they grow, these kittens become aggressive if their human caregiver does not wait on them quickly enough or tries to move away from an interaction. Why should this be?

Unfortunately, even when doing their best, human mothers are no substitute for the real thing. They may be able to provide an artificial milk that is suitable for the kitten, and even to wean it onto solid food when the time comes. However, when it comes to the subtle art of teaching appropriate feline behavior, they are often somewhat lacking. Scientists believe that the main problem is that, while the kitten may be successfully weaned nutritionally, behaviorally it has not learned to deal with frustration. Remember that, from about four weeks old, mother cats in the wild will start to bring in prey and will not offer food until the kittens start to demand it. The kittens must deal with the frustration of not getting what they want and transfer their energies on to the alternative food the mother has supplied. A person who is turning up every few hours and offering food, whether milk or solids, is not making them go through this development. No doubt this is a very simple representation of the complex learning required as kittens grow up. We are often not very good with our own kind when it comes to letting them know what they can and can't do – these kittens are probably close to what we might call a spoiled child. Whether these cats can be turned away from this aggressive response by behavioral therapy or whether they are difficult to change because that sensitive learning period has passed would be interesting to know.

I recently attended an evening seminar with demonstrations by the originator of horse listening, Monty Roberts. He has always advocated kindness and working with horses by understanding how they live as a herd, how they react, and how they interpret the things around them. The horse he worked with first was a hand-reared foal. He remarked that such a horse can be very difficult because during that feeding process it learns very quickly how to control its owner! People successfully provide the food but the lack of that species-specific maternal experience when it comes to teaching appropriate behavior is crucial. So it's not just cat owners who have such problems!

If you face the prospect of hand-rearing kittens, try to instigate a weaning process that will gradually expose them to frustrating experiences. It may be very useful to talk to a breeder with experience in this area who has learned what works and how this affects the temperament of kittens. It may be useful to put the kitten's food in feeders called puzzle feeders – as the kitten plays with the feeder (often in the form of a ball), the food comes out. In this way the owner is taken out of the food equation: he is not seen as such an important source of food.

THAT 15 PERCENT!

Just when you think you have cracked it, you find that there is a bit more to consider. Researchers have found that, while handling increased the confidence of kittens with people, there was a small proportion of kittens – around 15 percent – that did not respond to handling and remained resistant to it. This type of cat will not be satisfying for the kind of owner who wants a close and cuddly relationship with her cat but may be fine for someone who enjoys having a cat around in a more independent way. It is still uncertain as to whether these kittens that have had early handling do actually mellow in later years.

PULLING IT ALL TOGETHER

How can we interpret these clues as to how our kittens – and thus our cats – develop? How can we make use of them to ensure our pet cats are already primed and their brains educated to being good pets before they go to their new homes – that is, to pet owners who take them in from around seven weeks onward?

Healthy or sociable?

Sometimes ignorance is bliss where socializing kittens is concerned. The accidental litter born because a female kitten wasn't neutered in time is often cared for in the middle of busy family life. While owners may not even be aware of all the health hazards for young kittens, they are usually very eager to handle the kittens and they grow up in the middle of the household with all of its comings and goings. Thus they usually meet lots of people and get used to washing machines, computer noises, televisions, etc. – they understand human routines and normal chaos!

The overconscientious breeder, or the breeder churning out kittens for money, sometimes concentrates on the health aspects of kitten care to the detriment of socialization and habituation. It is not unreasonable to think that by isolating the kitten from other cats, or from people, you will safely prevent the spread of infectious disease and ensure a kitten's health. However, it is not quite so simple as that.

People sometimes refer to the process of socialization and habituation as immunizing the kitten against the problems that can arise from poor socialization. Socialization is essential if kittens and cats are to enjoy human contact rather than finding it oppressive and restrictive – which generates stress. It greatly reduces the potential problems of living closely with people as we want our pet cats to do. Similarly, stressed cats are much more vulnerable to disease, as stress seems to affect the immune system in some way. So a kitten that is kept in perfect health by missing out on socialization may actually be in more danger of health problems – both physical and emotional – as an adult. Of course, as with all things, both health and socialization are important. A healthy balance is the answer.

A Cat Is for Longer

You want a kitten – a beautiful little ginger one that will grow up like the cat you remember from your childhood. It turned up on your doorstep when you were small and moved in with the family. It was always around the house, slept in the warmest spot, and occasionally brought in live mice that the whole family had to try and catch (with great hilarity) and release in the yard. Ginger was a warm color and glows in your memories in warm spots in your home. It may be that you do find such a cat to fill Ginger's spot by the fire – or it may be a hard act to follow. Time to do a little profiling. A simple profile of you, your lifestyle, and your personality can give you some things to think about and a place to start weeding out some possibilities, if not to come up with the perfect solution. Start with the most obvious – your family circumstances.

HOW YOU LIVE

The number and ages of the people who live with you or who visit on a frequent basis will have an immediate impact on a kitten. If you live very quietly on your own and have few visitors, you will likely have time to spend with the kitten, patience, and a great interest in its every move. Much of your activity will be routine or regular, without great upset or noise. The kitten can have almost constant companionship if it wants. You may want a very outgoing kitten as a companion. Or you may be happy to take on a more nervous animal and gradually gain its confidence, carefully controlling its exposure to noise, activity, and other people.

You may be a single person or part of a couple who is out at work all day until late into the evening and who may go away for weekends quite regularly. The house may be uninhabited most of the time except late evenings, early mornings, and on weekends when you have friends visit. This can sometimes prove to be a difficult scenario. You want a cat that is confident and interactive so that it is happy to enjoy the time you are around and the hustle and bustle when friends are there. However, an outgoing and very interactive cat may not enjoy being left on its own all week. Here you may want to go for a confident, independent sort of cat rather than a very people-oriented one. You would probably avoid breeds such as Siamese or Burmese, which really enjoy doing almost everything with their owners, and go for a moggie or perhaps a British

Shorthair. Perhaps the most important thing to consider is whether you should actually get two cats instead of one. More on this later.

You may have a house full of young children where there is always lots of activity and often a great deal of noise! There will probably be someone around most of the time, be it yourself or a babysitter. While there may be a lot of people of all ages around, including unpredictable toddlers, there may not be a great deal of time to concentrate on the kitten's every whim or to make sure doors are kept shut – dangerous if the kitten is fearful and likely to bolt away. If it is unable to cope with the activity, it may hide under the furniture, or it may be accidentally stepped on or caught up in a tantrum.

Likewise the family with teenage children presents serious challenges for the nervous kitten – loud music, various new (and sometimes pretty weird) people coming and going at all times of the day, and probably not much routine. There may be quite a few adults or teens who take a great deal of interest in the kitten, but this may change; their attention may be variable, depending on what else is going on. Here again a confident kitten that is not too dependent, but is happy to fit in with the family, is needed.

Family scenarios usually require a kitten that is confident at the outset and robust enough to deal with frequent changes in companions, noise level, attention, and being left on its own. As we will see later, this is not necessarily a problem, and it is not difficult to find a kitten that will happily cope with it – it just needs a little planning. What will not work is a very nervous kitten in an environment where people do not have time, a consistent approach, or any control over the level of noise and activity in the home – a typical family picture!

Within these scenarios, what time do you, as perhaps the principal cat caregiver, have to spend on your new young charge? Having small children limits the time available and makes it unpredictable. This does not mean you cannot have a kitten; it just makes it a little more critical to choose the right one. Children want to hold and play with a kitten, and this needs to be supervised. The kitten also needs to be able to cope with some handling and attention. With many small minds caring so much about this little creature, you do not want to be in a situation where you have chosen an unhealthy animal that then dies, leaving children very upset indeed and you coping with the loss of the kitten as well as the emotions of the children. Your availability impacts not only companionship time for the kitten, but nursing time if it is required.

What kind of space do you have available for a cat? Do you live in a small tenth-floor apartment with no yard; do you have a rambling stately home; is your residence near a busy street or a quiet country road? What access could your cat have to the outdoors – free access, a fenced-in yard, no access at all, or do you intend to walk it on a lead?

Are you healthy and active, disabled, or even allergic? Being ill or disabled in no way means you should not take on a cat or kitten, it's just that you may have to think about practicalities of health and access, safety and energy. Even people who have lived with cats for many, many years forget the effort required to look after a kitten – it is like dealing with a flying toddler that is likely to get into all sorts of trouble if there is the slightest chance. You may decide it is safer for all concerned to get an older cat and leave kittens to those foolish enough to take one on! Allergies to cats is another of those great problems for people keen to take on a feline and is discussed later on.

In the family scenarios described previously we thought about the human part of the family, but what about resident animals? Dogs, other cats, and even rabbits are now indoor pets along with hamsters and cage birds. Having a kitten can have an effect on them, and they on it. I have had letters from people who want a kitten that will live safely with their bird, which they still intend to allow to have free access to fly. They want to be able to train the cat not to attack the bird and have them live together harmoniously. This is a very tall order for a top-of-the-chain carnivore that is triggered almost automatically into hunt mode by small moving creatures. It would be a strange kitten indeed that was not mesmerized by a fluttering bird and would not leap upon it if it happened to fly past. These people's faith in inter-species friendships is a lot greater than mine.

If you have other cats already, consider whether there is room for another feline in the home. Are you just a cat collector because you absolutely love them and another kitten needs a new home – surely squeezing an eighth or ninth cat in won't make any difference. The reason you have other cats may also influence not only your choice of kitten but also whether you should even be considering introducing another one.

Cats do live in groups or colonies – for example, on farms – and there is a structure to those colonies. The higher-ranking cats inhabit the territory at the center of the area near the sources of food and shelter, and those down the pecking order are pushed out to the edges. So cats do choose to live together even though their nearest ancestor, the African wildcat, is thought to be a solitary species. Our domestic cat is said to be a sociable animal, but it is choosy about its companions and whether it actually really wants any. In a free-living colony of unneutered cats, it is the females, their female kittens, and the young male kittens that really control who is allowed to stay. Within the cat colony there are what are called preferred associate relationships – other cats they prefer to spend time with. Cats that get along will groom, rub, and touch each other. There are also cats that could be classed as avoiders, which go out of their way not to be close to each other or spend time in each other's company – this seems to happen more between males and less between males and females. New cats are usually chased away. They may be taken into the colony if they persist past the initial attack and hang around long enough to take on the group smell and to gradually become absorbed. So the colony does have a choice as to who stays and who doesn't. Researchers studying a neutered colony of cats found that the cats that avoid each other do follow the same pattern seen in colonies of intact cats, suggesting that sexual competition between males and relationships between male and female potential mating partners are what drive these associations or avoidances.

This is not the same in a pet household, where humans choose a new individual and expect the others to like it or at least tolerate it. It would be like the government randomly choosing a person to live in your house and expecting you to accept him, get along with him, and even cuddle up on the couch in a couple of weeks (platonically, of course!). We shouldn't be surprised that adding a new cat to our household can be very stressful to the resident cat or cats. It may tip the balance of a very finely tuned relationship between the existing cats and set the household in turmoil. Sometimes it is best to be content with what you have and decide it is better not to bring in a new cat. That said, it is usually easier to introduce a kitten than a fully grown cat. Resident cats may not like them, but they are usually seen as less of a threat and tolerated a bit more – perhaps they smell young!

Emotions run even higher for the single cat kept permanently indoors in a small home and expected to adapt to a new kitten. It may feel that there is nowhere to hide and may not be used to dealing with huge changes to its lifestyle. While you may be feeling guilty that this older cat is left on its own a great deal and want it to have a friend, it may not agree with you, not only on whether it should have a companion, but on the one you have chosen. In these situations, introductions have to be organized quite carefully (see page 128).

If you already have a dog, bringing in a kitten should not be a problem in general, and it is often easier to introduce a kitten to a resident dog than to a resident cat. There is less competition and the two often become quite relaxed with each other, the cat rubbing around the dog and even sleeping with it. Some breeds and individuals are more likely to chase and even harm a new kitten and must be restrained and trained to tolerate the cat until it is established as part of the pack. In general the cat will turn out to be the boss of the relationship, as anyone with both canines and felines will tell you.

MOTIVATION

Why do you want a kitten? This is not a judgmental question – just another way of looking at your expectations and level of involvement. Wanting or expecting too much involvement can cause as many difficulties (sometimes more) than low involvement, again depending on the cat. There are, of course, many reasons for wanting a kitten – here are a few:

For the children to learn about animals and caring for them, or because the children want a pet and are pressuring you to get them one.

This is a sound reason for getting a kitten, provided you take responsibility for the children learning to handle and care for it correctly. You should also be willing to take over when they get bored or old enough to be distracted by the opposite sex or a new hobby. Luckily, cats are quite easy to keep so this should not be too much of a hardship.

For companionship for yourself, or because you want something to care for.

A cat is a wonderful companion and will indulge you in letting you care for it most readily!

You would like a dog but can't keep one.

Perhaps you should look at one of the more dog-like breeds. These may be a bit more high-maintenance than moggies or some laid-back breeds, but they may more than satisfy your wish for a dog within the space or time constraints that prevent you from having one in the first place. You will soon become a converted ailurophile (cat lover), and such converts are often the most enthusiastic of all!

To have an unusual breed to show off to your friends.

As long as you are a cat lover first and foremost, then there are indeed some unusual breeds that you might have a look at. Unlike dogs, however, cats are more likely to be a private pleasure reserved for close friends and colleagues to meet in our homes – not for attracting glances when walking down the street with a large or strange breed of dog.

For showing and breeding.

There is certainly one way of sharing your breed with others and that is to show it at cat shows. There are many local shows and larger ones with moggie categories as well as pedigrees if you have an interest in showing. Breeding is another matter altogether and you need to undertake a great deal of research on the breed, the breed lines, and the individual you choose before you go forward. Some people may think that they can make a lot of money this way. Done properly – avoiding overcrowding, ensuring you have time to socialize kittens properly, providing all the vaccinations, etc. – does not leave much room for large profit. What it does bring is large responsibility. You choose the cats you are mating and are therefore responsible for the inherited temperament of the kittens and for trying to avoid inherited diseases. You are also solely responsible for their socialization. All of these factors contribute to how the kitten tackles life – nervously or with confidence, and whether it is prone to illness or good health. You also have to find them responsible new owners. Quite a responsibility in all.

**To give an unwanted kitten a home –
the feel-good factor.**

As we have seen, many, many cats come from an animal shelter – perhaps a third of all cats. Most will be moggies, although many of the breed clubs organize themselves to take on and re-home cats of that particular breed. This does make sense because they know the details of the breed and are perhaps able to match a new owner to a particular cat's needs. Some well-run rescue organizations do an excellent job with cats and they are striving to improve the way they work all the time. There are some, however, who do not and these are to be avoided – more of this in Chapter 5. Many people like to feel that they have given a home to a kitten that did not have one and have helped reduce the number of homeless animals.

As company for your other cat.

This is a difficult one and could blow up in your face! Many cats are very happy on their own and would rather stay that way. If you have had a cat that you know is relaxed with other cats around and has accepted others readily, then you might have an easy time. Otherwise, take it slowly and make careful introductions – see Chapter 7. Of course, many people do introduce new kittens with ease, but don't expect it. If you feel that your cat may be left alone for long periods, you may want to consider getting two kittens at the outset – siblings would be the easiest option. Quite often owners use the idea of getting their cat a companion as an excuse to get another one. There is no shame in wanting more cats – we all love them. Just admit it is really for you, and don't expect your cat to love it at first sight.

You have always liked cats and now have a chance to own one of your own.

Hurrah!

WHY A KITTEN RATHER THAN A CAT?

Kittens are adorable, hard work, entertaining, often destructive, and usually delightful. It is a joy to own one at least once in your life. Many people take on older cats, often because there are many more of them needing a good home than kittens, find homes more easily because of their appeal. It is hard work – they keep you on your toes like any baby or toddler. Indeed, many people taking on a kitten for the first time after many years of owning adult cats comment that they had forgotten what hard work it is!

Some aspects of your personality may also affect the type of kitten you choose, or should choose, and the lifestyle you will have with it, such as whether it goes outside or stays indoors.

Are you patient?

Kittens do require patience, and if you are taking on a long-haired cat you may have to spend a great deal of time grooming – Persians especially will not be able to look after their coats on their own.

Are you house-proud – do you mind accidents, scratched furniture or wallpaper, hair on the furniture, litter boxes, etc.?

Tales of kittens climbing up curtains are based on truth – they may well shin up anything they can and in the process knock off ornaments or pull down curtains that are not securely fixed! Remember when you had children or friends visiting with children and put all the valuables away? Time to do it again. Cats do shed hair, and long-haired cats shed a lot of it.

Are you overprotective?

Some people could not bear to take on a cat and then let it face the risks of going outside. They may want to keep it indoors – but there are things to consider if taking this option, both at the outset and as it grows. These considerations are covered further in Chapter 9.

What sort of owner will you be? What do you want from your cat? Do you want a close relationship, or are you happy to live with it and respect it for its independence? Owners can be dissatisfied with their cat because they have unrealistic expectations of how it might live with them or because the cat does not fit what they want. One such story was told to me recently by a member of a rescue organization. A very nice lady came in and adopted a beautiful tortoiseshell-and-white cat. She brought it back the next day because, as an artist, she could not cope with the fact that the markings on its legs were not symmetrical – she had even considered coloring it in! Suggestions by staff that she could use artistic license when she was painting it fell on deaf ears!

OK, self-analysis finished – you have thought it through and are ready to choose your kitten. It may have seemed a little labored but, if a dog is for life, then a cat is for even longer! Many cats live for fourteen years and upward, so they are potentially with you for a long time, sometimes longer than children. What are the choices available to you?

4

Your Choices

Once you have decided you want a kitten, there are actually quite a few decisions to be made before you go down a particular path in getting it. Do you want a pedigree or a moggie? Are you after a particular breed? How many kittens do you want, what sex do you want them to be, and when should you actually aim to become a cat owner?

TIMING

Once the decision has been made to get a kitten, it's only human to want to get one NOW. You would be excused for wanting to snuggle down with the little thing and love it to pieces – kittens are irresistible. However, you do need to be sensible – boring though it often is! We often want a kitten during the winter months when it is dark early in the evening and the thought of having a warm cat snuggled up on our lap is very appealing. However, this is often the time when there are the fewest kittens around. Even though we can provide our pet cats with all the food and shelter they need, they still follow rhythms that would allow them to survive if they lived as wild animals. The ability to breed is switched off in female cats as the days get shorter and winter approaches – very sensible to avoid having young to feed when much of your prey is hibernating or avoiding the cold and is rather scarce. As the days start to get longer again early in the year (in the northern hemisphere), female cats will start to come into season and call for mates. After a gestation period of nine weeks, kittens are born in the early spring – perfect timing for their mothers to take advantage of the activity and breeding of small rodents and birds. These prey provide adequate nutrition for producing milk and for weaning growing kittens. Of course, pet cats don't have to rely on this natural source of food, but they still answer to the seasonal rhythms. Female cats can have two or three litters over the spring and summer, and the last one may be as late as October. Some rescue organizations, to whom it falls to find homes for thousands of kittens each year, feel that our warming climate, whatever its root cause, is actually lengthening the breeding season for cats, and it is more common now to find kittens throughout the year. However, the largest numbers needing homes are still present in spring and summer.

Some pedigree cats seem to breed all year round quite naturally, and the body can indeed be fooled into coming into season if it is given extra light. Therefore, it can be easier to find pedigree kittens during the winter months.

Most animal welfare organizations dissuade people from taking on kittens (or other animals) over the Christmas period because it is a time when the festivities, visiting friends and relatives, excited children, and liberal amounts of alcohol can make our houses a little unsettled! Routines disappear, there are decorations and lights everywhere, and small kittens could be forgotten in all of the activities. However, this said, it is also a time when many people have a week or even two off work and may be an ideal time to give a new kitten extra care and attention as it settles in. Not every home is chaotic over Christmas!

You do need to have time to settle in a new kitten. It makes sense to take some time off or to ensure that your new charge arrives on a holiday so that you both have some time to get to know each other. If no one is home during the normal working day with the kitten, then a visit at lunchtime to check up on it would be ideal provided your job is nearby. Otherwise a friend or neighbor might check up on the kitten for the first week or so.

Avoid getting a kitten just before you go on vacation, as you will have to put it into a cattery just after it has gotten used to your home and routines. It is also not wise to leave a kitten to be fed only once daily by a neighbor – kittens tend to get up to a lot of mischief indoors or out, or they may decide to go in search of company. A good cattery is a much safer option.

Another combination that can be a little stressful is that of new baby and new kitten! Each young thing deserves individual attention, and human babies are all-consuming. Parents expecting their first child may not realize that "all-consuming" means just what it says – there is no easy way to do it! It is also a very stressful time for new moms and dads, and they worry about how everything might affect the new baby. Better to wait until the baby is six to nine months old at least. Remember too that small children, even if not very mobile, are excellent at grabbing … and holding on. Children and kittens can and do mix very well, but children need to be controlled and taught to treat kittens with respect.

So choose your time carefully. Give your new kitten a chance to get to know you and your home and for the residents there – humans, dogs, cats, and even rabbits – to get used to it too. (There is more on introductions in Chapter 7.) These can be vitally important in assimilating your new kitten into your home as smoothly as possible.

PEDIGREE OR MOGGIE?

You may already have decided that you want a particular breed of cat because you have seen one you like or you have come to know one through friends or relatives. Or you may be a fan of good old mixed-blood moggies and wouldn't consider anything else. Your choice may then be based on the individual looks and the character of cats of a particular pedigree – in which case you can flick forward to the next chapter. However, perhaps you have always had moggies and are rather tempted to try a breed to see if there really is any difference or because you decide you want a certain coat color or length. Unlike dog owners, who often seem to favor one breed above all others, cat lovers often have a cat of a particular breed and a moggie, enjoying the differences in personality and form as well as the similarities of feline behaviors. Individual cats do vary widely in their personalities and these variations can span the breed differences too, but there are tendencies within the breeds to exhibit certain characteristics or degrees of behavior that make them a little different.

Some of the stronger breed tendencies will be outlined a little later, but I would like to stick my neck out and generalize very broadly about some differences between pedigrees and moggies. If you have read the earlier chapters you will know that the difference between a friendly cat and a non-friendly cat can all boil down to how it is handled and brought up in those very few days between two and seven weeks old. Given a level playing field of an excellent breeder, be it for moggie or pedigree, where kittens get the same handling and attention, would there be any difference? Until recently I might have said no, but I am becoming more convinced that many of the breeds are much more interactive and people-oriented than moggies. This is not to say that one is any better or worse, it just sets up a different type of relationship. Many people want a cat because it is independent and doesn't hang on their every breath or activity; they want to be able to go out without worry and know the cat won't mind at all. They don't want to feel guilty that the cat is not always the center of attention when they deal with the kids, the house, their job, and hobbies.

Which breed?

If you think you might like a particular breed, then do some research and try to find somebody experienced in that breed who can tell you about it. Good breeders will be happy to discuss this with you – more of this in Chapter 5. There are over thirty breeds to choose from, but there are probably ten that could be discussed with some confidence in terms of personality.

Typically a small percentage of the cats owned are pedigree cats. Unlike dog breeds, which differ hugely in size and shape, cats are pretty much the same; some a little smaller and some a little larger. However, the difference may be a factor of one or two, rather than ten found when comparing the extremes of canine breeds.

Within the different breeds of cat there can be very different rules about coat color or pattern. For example, Russian Blues come mostly in blue (actually a steely gray color), although I have a feeling there is also a rarer white version. Some breeds have a limited number of colors, such as the different point colors of the Siamese (the term "point" refers to face, tail, and legs). And some breeds include an unlimited variety of colors and patterns but specify a particular body shape and coat length, which is known as the "breed standard." Most dog breeds have one look, such as the Golden Retriever, or a limited number of variations, such as yellow, black, or chocolate Labradors. Cats can have a much more varied coat pattern and color than dogs, as well as three basic coat lengths. The density of the coat can vary tremendously too. While most moggies will fall into the short-haired or semi-long-haired categories, within the pedigrees the Persian has a hugely dense, long coat and the Sphynx has only a fine down of hair, which gives it the appearance of baldness.

Your cat's coat type and length do require some thought. While many people may see the lush coat of the Persian and think that it seems very exotic and beautiful, they are probably unaware of the hard work that goes into maintaining it in that form. The cat itself cannot maintain this much coat in the clean and untangled condition we so love to see and which cats seem to yearn for. So many Persians become victims of their own coats, their owners either unwilling or unable to groom them and the tangles becoming larger and larger until the whole coat is matted. The only way to remedy this is to take the cat to the veterinarian for a general anesthetic and to have the coat cut or shorn off to start again. This much hair is also likely to find its way in copious amounts onto furniture and clothes, which may not suit the meticulously minded unless they are very conscientious cleaners.

An easier way to enjoy a flowing coat without providing so much care is to choose what is known as a semi-longhair – breeds such as the Maine Coon or the Norwegian Forest Cat, the Birman or the Ragdoll. While these breeds will need a helping hand with their coats, they do quite a bit of the work themselves. Problems often occur when seeds or sticky things get stuck in the coat and form the core of a knot. Having owned a semi-long-haired moggie originally called Smokie but later changed to Debris on account of the ring of bits and pieces he left behind (usually on the cream duvet) after a grooming session, I can say that I am not really a long-haired-cat sort of person! If you don't think that even a small amount of regular grooming is up your alley, or realistically speaking you don't have the time, even if you wanted to, then aim for a short-haired breed that is perfectly in control of its own coat maintenance. Sleek and shiny, that's how I like them!

Another reason people consider coat length is if someone in the household is allergic to cats. However, this is usually based on the incorrect assumption that it is the hair that causes the allergic reaction. To be scientifically correct, it is not. The allergen – the protein that causes the allergic reaction of sneezing or wheezing in some people – is found in the cat's saliva. When it grooms, the cat coats the hair with saliva, spreading the allergen onto its coat. Even practically bald breeds will groom themselves and thus could cause an allergic reaction. However, it does seem that long hair causes a greater reaction – this may just be because there is more hair and therefore more allergen both on the cat and in the environment. There are lots of allergens in our environment, not just from cats but from dust mites and pollen, etc. Decreasing the total volume will help the sufferer, as it lessens the cumulative effect. Replacing carpets with solid flooring such as wood, tiles, or laminates that can be easily cleaned, choosing furniture that is upholstered with leather or leatherlike material, using blinds instead of curtains, and doing without cushions or covering them with plastic or leather material will all help to reduce the allergen load. Vacuum with an air filter, open windows as much as possible, and wear clothes that do not hold on to allergens. As well as often being itchy for those with sensitive skin, wool apparently holds up to ten times more allergens than cotton or synthetic materials.

Remove excess hair from the cat with daily brushing – outside so that the hair can blow away – and make sure grooming clothes or an apron do not come into the house except for frequent washing. Experts also advise that the cat be bathed weekly – while some cats may tolerate this, others will not. Bathing could become a difficult and sometimes dangerous struggle for all concerned, and it can take away many of the joys of owning the cat in the first place. Keep the cat out of the bedroom and don't hug it closely; washing your hands after stroking will help too. There are also several products available that can be wiped over the cat that are supposed to reduce allergens.

Many allergic people don't want to live without a cat – the measures above may help to reduce symptoms such as sneezing and wheezing. For some it does not work – allergies are a complex problem and we are still learning. Perhaps their only hope is an allergen-free cat – one is actually being genetically engineered at present, and no doubt there will be plenty of cat lovers with several thousand dollars to spare who will want one.

More about breeds

I have no intention of going into detail here about all thirty or so breeds that are available. Some of the twenty most popular are: British Shorthair, Persian, Siamese, Burmese, Bengal, Birman, Ragdoll, Maine Coon, Oriental Shorthair, Exotic Shorthair, Devon and Cornish Rex, Asian Shorthair, Tonkinese, Abyssinian, Norwegian Forest Cat, Russian Blue, Somali, Egyptian Mau, Korat, and Balinese. A good cat encyclopedia will give you details on the body size and shape, eye color, ear position, length of coat, and the various colors each breed may or may not come in. They are all beautiful.

If you are after a very long-haired cat that needs lots of brushing, the Persian may be for you. However, it does have a very flat face; as with dog breeds in which the muzzle has been shortened considerably, head shape changes have to occur in order to fit in all the relevant pieces in a smaller volume. Hence the eyes of the Persian, like those of the Pekinese and other flat-faced dog breeds, are not deep in the sockets, as they are in longer-faced breeds, but pushed outwards. For this reason they may not drain in the same way as other cats' eyes – the fluid that is required to keep the eye surface moist may not drain away through the tear duct but spill out and over the face. Some Persians may need their eyes wiped frequently. They may also have jaw problems because the top and lower jaw do not fit together as they should. And, with a much shorter nose, they may have trouble breathing if they have an infection or are stressed. The original Persian did have a rather nice nose – it is a shame that we always seem to go too far and push breeds to the extreme; we should have learned from looking at the various dog breeds that such extremes have problems. I must admit to not being a great Persian fan – as I have already admitted, grooming is not really for me, nor is eye-wiping or cleaning up dirty hair under cats' tails. So with apologies to Persian lovers, I would suggest that most busy people who like long coats might prefer a semi-long-haired breed, which still has plenty of hair but is a bit easier to care for. Many Persians end up in animal shelters because their owners just didn't realize they needed so much grooming. I take my hat off to those owners who manage to keep that fantastic coat in tip-top condition.

If you do want a Persian, then it is imperative to find a good breeder who can make sure you get a fit and healthy kitten and give you guidance on grooming, eye wiping, etc. And just one more thing: if you are still convinced this is the breed for you, ask the breeder about PKD – polycystic kidney disease, an inherited disease that affects around 40 percent of Persians and in which cysts (fluid-filled holes) form within the kidney and increase in size as the cat gets older. Some cats with these cysts do seem to have pretty normal life spans – over eleven or twelve years. Many are affected, however, and die at around seven or eight years, and some at only two or three years. Breeders should find out whether their breeding stock is affected by having the kidneys scanned by ultrasound (which will show any cysts). Clear parents cannot pass on the gene, so kittens should be unaffected. Ask the breeder if the parents have been tested and if they have certificates to show that no cysts were found. Just as I am writing this, I hear that a genetic test for PKD is well on the way, so there may be an additional way to test for the disease in the near future.

Many people love their Persians – they are beautiful, they are pretty laid-back, and they are not noisy. Many people also want to give a cat that high level of care and enjoy the grooming – it's just as well we don't all like the same thing.

Strangely enough, if you like the chunkier shape of the body, the flatter face, and the undemanding temperament of the Persian but don't like all that hair, then you may be interested in what is called the Exotic Shorthair – it is really a short-haired Persian.

Of the most popular breeds that are classed as semi-longhair (they lack the very thick undercoat of the Persians), you have the Birman, Ragdoll, Maine Coon, Norwegian Forest Cat, Somali, and Balinese to think about.

The Birman has white feet and dark points (face, tail, and legs) on a paler body and is said to be intelligent, gentle, and quiet. The Ragdoll also has a silky medium-length coat and is said to enjoy being picked up (I suspect individuals vary, though, as would be expected). Two of these breeds that have recently become very popular are the Maine Coon (said to be the largest breed) and the Norwegian Forest Cat. Both developed a long, thick waterproof coat to survive cold winters and come in a variety of colors and patterns. The Somali is the long-haired version of the Abyssinian, and the Balinese is the longer-haired version of the Siamese. Both are said to be intelligent and lively.

Another popular breed, especially overseas, is the British Shorthair, in particular the silver tabby and British Blue versions of the breed. The British Shorthair is a good, sturdy cat with a sensible, friendly disposition. I do tend to think of it as a kind of posh moggie – it comes in many colors and is rounder and chunkier but still has that moggie common sense and isn't very noisy or too demanding. It does come in some very lovely colors and patterns that you don't usually get with moggies – the stronger tabby colors and patterns: colors like blue (a beautiful silvery gray) and even color pointed like the Siamese.

Then we come to Siamese and Oriental Shorthairs, and I must admit to being somewhat biased here. I have owned a Siamese or Oriental for many years (along with moggies) and have a soft spot for their angular bodies and chatty nature. They are bright and sometimes even dog-like in nature – some enjoy retrieving and can be trained to walk on a harness and lead. Their ability to be trained is probably a result of their enjoyment of attention and interaction with their owners. They may not be any more intelligent than other cats, but can be very motivated to do things that keep them in touch with their owners – hence training them is a lot easier. Orientals have a solid coat pattern instead of the darker-colored points well known as Siamese patterning, but a similar slender and angular body shape. Both are energetic and playful and will demand attention.

Another breed that thrives on human attention is the Burmese. It comes in a variety of colors, from the most commonly known brown to blue and tortoiseshell. It has a rounder appearance than the Siamese and is energetic and confident. Burmese have strong characters and need an owner who is happy to give them time and attention – they can be quite demanding.

If you can't decide between a Siamese and a Burmese, you could go for a Tonkinese – developed from a cross between the two breeds, it looks like a chunkier version of a traditional Siamese and is said to be slightly less demanding than its original parent breeds.

Every so often a new breed comes along and becomes popular quickly. One such breed is the Bengal. It is said that it was originally bred as part of a research project to find cats that might show immunity to feline leukemia virus (FeLV) and is the result of mating the domestic cat with the Asian Leopard Cat. The resulting cats were, unfortunately, as susceptible to FeLV as any others, but looked very pretty, with strong spotted or marbled markings on a pale coat background. Initially they were also quite fearful, as the Asian Leopard Cat would, like most other wild cats, wish to avoid human contact and live hidden from sight. However, despite many breeders jumping on the bandwagon because of the increasing demand for these very pretty cats, subsequent generations seem to have developed as confident, playful, and athletic cats. I hope it is a case of the good breeders steering the breed through the demand and developing friendly and confident characteristics. I have to admit these cats do seem to have turned out OK and look very beautiful – however, we do have enough beautiful colors and patterns in the cats we already have. I feel that crossing them with wild cousins is not the way to go and hope that those who like to experiment will desist from other similar cross-breeding.

The Devon and Cornish Rex are interesting breeds. Both were developed independently but have similar fine hair with a rippled appearance, which looks a bit sparser than a normal cat coat. Both have large eyes and ears, with the Devon having very large, low-set ears that give it the appearance of a pixie. Rexes are said to be intelligent, friendly, and rather naughty.

Another relatively new breed is the Asian Shorthair – it is related to the Burmese, comes in a wide range of colors (many of which are very beautiful), and has yellow-green eyes. It is said to be intelligent and curious but less demanding than the Burmese.

If you are looking for a cat that will be friendly to you but might be a little reticent around strangers, then the Abyssinian may be for you. It also has an unusual coat that is ticked (each hair has at least two dark bands), giving it an appearance similar to that of a wild rabbit and presumably like that of its ancestor the African Wildcat.

Two blue cats next – the Russian Blue and the Korat. They have different body and head shapes, but both have that beautiful silver-gray coat we call blue. Both are said to have gentle natures and to be intelligent and affectionate.

In our top twenty that just leaves the Egyptian Mau, whose beautiful, randomly spotted coat pattern gives it a striking appearance, similar to that of the silver tabby we all love.

Of course looks are important and everyone finds something different attractive, but I like to consider personality too. Many cats of the breeds mentioned above will have a similar personality, but some breeds may be a bit more demanding than others in terms of attention, interaction, or care. There are also some less common breeds, such as the almost hairless Sphynx, the spotted Ocicat, the newly introduced La Perm, and many others. Do your homework and find out before you commit your heart – and your wallet! Think too about the breed – the Munchkin, which is like the cat version of the short-legged Corgi, may be a novelty, but it is not a good addition to the world of cats. If you do decide to go ahead, read Chapter 5 about finding a good breeder.

HOW MANY KITTENS?

I always feel rather gleeful when I bring up the idea of taking on two kittens rather than one. I suppose it is because I would be delighted, having got over all of the hurdles associated with actually deciding to take on a kitten, to find that there were no more hurdles (or only small ones) when it came to changing one to two!

One argument against, and the most obvious, is the increase in cost. If you are going the pedigree route, then it will be twice the cost of a kitten to begin with, plus (no matter what the breeding) increased costs of neutering, feeding, vaccination (although pedigree cats should come fully vaccinated), medical expenses, insurance, etc. The money argument may be a strong one, and if you feel you can't afford two and are only confident that you can care properly for one, one will be absolutely fine.

Why suggest two when I have said that many cats like to be on their own and will resist another cat coming into the household? It is exactly this reasoning that points to getting two cats together at the same time. Many of us who have only one cat soon realize that we would actually like to get another but worry about how they will get along and how our original cat will react – in reality they might not like each other at all. Kittens within a litter do form bonds with each other – they are together during that sensitive period of socialization when cats are able to form bonds among themselves. They often stay together until they are two or three months old, playing and grooming and being very relaxed together. They stand a very good chance of getting along for their entire lives because these social ties persist (if they are kept together). So the easiest option is to take on siblings.

A second option may be to take on two kittens of about the same age from different sources at the same time – there is still a good chance of them getting along well, although not so high a chance as there would be with siblings. However, be aware of the health implications of this – both kittens need to be healthy and not a potential disease risk for each other. You might want to discuss age and vaccination status with your veterinarian if you want to mix kittens that are not fully vaccinated before they come together.

OK. So getting two cats together means they will get along better than trying to introduce one later on when you realize that your home needs another feline. Anything else? Aside from double the beauty, fun, and cuddle value for owners, getting two together does something very important. It relieves the guilt factor associated with leaving a single kitten alone all day and worrying that it might be lonely; two kittens can keep each other company, play, or curl up together and ease the conscience greatly!

Will getting two kittens together consume the cats' affections and make them focus on each other rather than you? This does not seem to happen, perhaps because cats are not pack animals – or perhaps because they do not compartmentalize their affections but share them with their owners quite happily. This is especially true if one or both kittens are confident and outgoing – they tend to be generous with their affections. If one kitten is a little more nervous than the other, it may learn to follow and behave like the confident sibling. Remember, kittens learn lots by just watching what other cats do and how they react.

Companionship will also be of particular help in those first few days when the kittens are in their new home. Everything else in their lives has changed drastically, which can be quite a shock to the system.

You can see that I am pretty keen on the two-rather-than-one approach – twice the trouble perhaps, but the fun factor is squared.

WHICH SEX?

I have changed my mind over the years about the sex question. However, whichever sex of kitten you choose is not going to make a vast amount of difference as long as you neuter your kitten(s) early enough. Many of the differences between the sexes are shaped by hormones that dominate cats' reproductive lives. Unneutered mature males will mark, patrol, and defend their territory with great enthusiasm and will roam for many miles in search of females to mate with. Unneutered females will come into season at around six months old and call (a particular loud meow accompanied by rolling and other sexual behaviors) every two weeks or so unless they become pregnant. Females can have two or even three litters during the breeding season. When the shortening of the days changes the hormonal cocktail, the urge to breed stops until day length increases again (thus preventing birth of kittens during the winter when food is scarce and weather is cold). By neutering kittens before the influences of sex hormones kick in, we find that there is not a great deal of difference between the behaviors of males and females. Thus, if you are just getting one kitten and you have no other cats at home, it doesn't really matter which sex you choose.

What if you get two kittens – is there a best combination of sexes? Having spent a fascinating weekend listening to David MacDonald from Oxford University, an expert on animal behavior and conservation, talk about the behavior of kittens within feral colonies on farms, I have altered my thinking a little on this. MacDonald was one of the first people to look at the behavior of our domestic cats in this way. He has also done a great deal of work with the behavior of lions and has noted some similarities between these feline cousins. While our domestic cats do not hunt together, they do have a social structure that is beneficial to the group as a whole, and the group does rely on the females within it. With lions, there is a kinship between males that can persist into adulthood where allegiances between male lions may make the difference between taking over a pride or losing it. In our pet cats these male coalitions do not occur; indeed, adult intact males will avoid each other. However, MacDonald did note that male kittens do stay closer to and interact more with other male kittens than with female ones. Kittens of either sex preferred to be with related kittens rather than those that were not related. Can we use this to help us in our choice? Neutered male cats do seem to get along well, especially if related, so getting two males may be an option for a stable, good-natured relationship.

What about the girls? In the same feral situation, you will find that the group is organized around the females – mother cats and their daughters. Males will leave when they are old enough, and toms will come and go. Thus, related females seem to have strong bonds. Unrelated females will not be welcomed, which may be relevant if you are considering which sex of kitten to get if you already have a resident cat.

I used to suggest getting one kitten of each sex if you wanted two kittens, so that there was less chance of sexual competition, but perhaps now I would recommend two of the same sex.

What if you already have a resident cat? If you already have a resident male (neutered), it probably doesn't make much difference whether you introduce a male or a female. However, if you have a female cat and want to introduce a new kitten, you may want to try a male kitten. In my experience, female cats are much more protective of their core territory (your house) than males. In the wild, they would have a lot to lose if they let in another female who would compete for the food and for the best nest site, especially if she was not related – there is value in cooperating to preserve the genes of offspring and close relatives, but not those of strangers.

However, as with everything feline, individuals will always defy trends, so there is no predicting how your particular cat may react to a new kitten, of either sex. It is likely to react less aggressively to a kitten than to an adult cat, perhaps because it is not direct competition – yet! The choice of the sex of your kitten is not crucial. Introductions are probably as important, if not more so, as is the socialization your cat and kitten both received before you had them – some help that, then!

Sexing your kitten

It is surprising how often mistakes are made with the sex of kittens. If you are in any doubt you should ask your veterinarian (who will check prior to neutering anyway).

To tell the difference between the sexes you will need to lift the tail and look at the genitals. In the male, less than a half inch (1 cm) below the anus is the opening of the prepuce with the scrotum immediately above this. The anus and prepuce appear like two "dots." In the female, the vulva is a vertical slit that is almost joined to the anus, like a letter "i."

5

Finding
Your Kitten

There are many and various ways to obtain a kitten, and the one you choose may depend on whether you want a pedigree or a moggie kitten, whether you have a friend who needs a home for a litter, or how impatient you are to get one!

As discussed earlier, probably about a third of our pet cats come from rescue organizations, although most of these are probably young or adult cats rather than kittens. Shelters often stagger under the weight of kittens in the spring and summer but may not have so many at other times of the year. Likewise these times of the year see numerous notices in the veterinarian's office or the newsstands offering kittens free to good homes. These are usually the product of accidental litters – the owners of last year's kittens have failed to neuter their female cats early enough and the kittens have proved that they are rather more mature than their owners realized! Pet shops too may offer kittens for sale – more of this later. And then there are the breeders of pedigree kittens. There are things to note if you obtain your kitten from any of these sources, and being forewarned and knowledgable is very helpful in trying to make the best choice for you, your family, and the kitten in question.

THE PEDIGREE ROUTE

Having thought long and hard about the breed you want by researching in books or on the Internet, it is well worth visiting a cat show and looking at the different breeds in the flesh. The people there will be able to give you an idea about some of the breeds' habits or idiosyncrasies, grooming requirements, etc. It is much easier to believe just how much grooming is required for a Persian when you see it close up and realize how thick the coat is. Owners at the show will be able to give you tips on the best grooming equipment and techniques from their experiences. Ask a few people – those who care about their particular breed will not just sing its praises but will be truthful about some of the less-easy-to-live-with characteristics of the cats. They will also want to ensure that you as a potential owner are the right type of person to take on that breed. They may feel it needs company or may explain how demanding or interactive that breed tends to be. All breeders will not be experts – some may give downright dreadful advice, others will be very helpful, so talk to a few and choose those who seem to talk sense. You may even find a breeder whose queen is having a litter and be able to arrange to see the kittens at a later date. You will not be able to buy a kitten directly at the show.

If you can't get to a show, you might want to contact the person or organization sponsoring the event. He or she should be able to give you information about breed clubs – groups of individuals who are interested in a similar breed or color. You can call them directly, find information on their web site, or request information via e-mail. There are also cat magazines at the newsstand and local newspapers with lists of kittens for sale.

A good breeder will not sell kittens via pet shops because he or she will care deeply about who buys the kittens and will be willing to take them back if there are any problems. They will want to talk to potential owners directly. It is also very important for new owners to see the kittens and their mother to assess her personality and what she is passing on to her kittens.

There are several reasons why you might want a pedigree kitten. You may simply want a kitten as a pet, you may want to show it at cat shows, or you might want to breed from it yourself. You will need to decide which category you fall into before you buy the kitten because breeders will often offer kittens as pets or for breeding, and they will differ in some aspects.

If you want to show your kitten or cat, then you will need to find out more about the breed standard. This is a list of descriptions of what is acceptable for that particular breed – coat color, length, or pattern, shape of the head, set of the ears, body size and composition, color of eyes, etc. There is no point in buying a kitten with a fault – perhaps a spot of white in the wrong place – if this is going to be important. Show-quality kittens are expensive to buy, and you should talk to breeders who have a track record for show cats.

If you want to breed kittens, you may be able to buy a cat that conforms to the breed standard. A cat with one or two points that are not quite up to standard, but which has many other good qualities, could also produce excellent kittens. Again, you will need to do your homework about what is important in the breed and look into different breeding lines. There is much that you can find out and lots you will learn later from experience!

Most of us, if we do want a pedigree kitten because we like the look or temperament we have investigated, are not that bothered if it has a small fault in its coat coloring, if its ears are not quite big enough, or if it fails in some other detail necessary to win on the show bench. What we do not want, however, is the kind of fault that can affect the kitten's health, such as an upper and lower jaw that do not fit together properly, or teeth that are out of alignment and may cause problems. We do not wish to breed it but to have it as a beloved pet. Pet-quality kittens are probably less expensive than show- or breeding-quality kittens, but they should be healthy and just as delightful – it does not mean that they are of inferior quality healthwise. You can always ask the breeder to explain the different types within the litter to you. Don't try to fool the breeder by pretending you want a pet-quality animal when you really want one to show or breed from (pet-standard are usually cheaper than show- or breed-quality kittens). There may be reasons why you cannot use it for these purposes, and you may be disappointed later on.

Having found a breeder who has kittens, what do you do? The first contact is likely to be by phone. Explain what you want, the number and sex of the kittens you are interested in, or simply ask what is available and try to judge the breeder as she (it is quite likely to be a she) talks to you. Good breeders will be an excellent source of information and will be happy to guide if you let them. Ask about the age of the kittens, whether they are vaccinated, whether they are registered, whether they have special needs (such as grooming), and the cost. Ask about registration even if you are never likely to use it except to put the paperwork in the back of the drawer and forget about it. Registering costs the breeder money and proves that the kitten's mother and father are both registered cats. It can help you avoid people who are just breeding kittens for profit without any records or knowledge about what they are doing. If you want to check the price quoted to you, ask the breed-club secretary, who will be able to give you the range of acceptable prices and make sure that you are not taken for a ride just because you are not familiar with the breeding world. There are always people out there who will take advantage of customers who do not have all the facts at their fingertips, so do your homework. If the breeder sounds interested in your home and how you will care for the kitten and tries to ensure that you have made a good choice for your circumstances, you know she is not just out for a sale at any cost. Allow your instincts to guide you; use common sense. Remember, just because someone says she is a breeder or has been breeding cats for twenty years, it does not necessarily mean she is an expert. Do your homework, find out the facts, and then judge the breeder on the answers you get to some questions you already know the answers to. There are some excellent caring and very skilled breeders out there – make sure you find one.

Ask about the breeder's household – are kittens reared in the main house or an outdoor shed; have they met dogs and children; and are they happy with the sounds of the vacuum cleaner, the television, the doorbell, etc.? It will be very important to you to have a confident, well-socialized kitten that will adapt easily to your home.

Oftentimes breeders of pedigree kittens will have their kittens vaccinated before they go to their new homes. This is to give them maximum protection against infectious diseases that they may encounter in the big world outside the breeder's establishment. Vaccinations against feline enteritis and cat flu (rhinotracheitis) are recommended.

There are other vaccinations (see Chapter 10), but these are the essentials. Kittens need to have both injections on the vaccination course (one at about eight weeks and one about two weeks later), and they will not feel the full effect of the immunity until about a week after the second vaccination. For this reason pedigree kittens are usually about thirteen weeks old when they are ready to go to their new homes. The breeder should be able to give you the vaccination certificate, which is signed by a veterinarian. This means that breeders are totally responsible for the socialization of their kittens. The whole "sensitive" period occurs before the kittens are rehoused so it is too late for new owners to do much about it. Therefore, when you have arranged to see the kittens be ready to ask questions about health and socialization. On your visit, observe and ask about how the kittens have been raised thus far.

This brings up the topic of health versus socialization, which you might want to consider before venturing into breeders' homes, where they seem to have all the answers. When you are breeding kittens, there are numerous things to take account of. There are also lots of things that can go wrong. Some of the infectious diseases that can pass from one cat to another, or from the mother to the kittens, are quite tricky to contend with. Some are viruses that are very common but can cause serious disease in kittens; others are bacterial infections, which can also cause problems. There is no doubt that these organisms love to wreak havoc, and where there are lots of cats, they will thrive. Thus, hygiene is very important, as are healthy breeding animals and vaccination where appropriate.

What does this mean in practical terms? It means that cats should not be kept in vast numbers and that breeders should only have one or two litters on the go at any one time. When you go to see the breeder you should not find yourself having to step back as you enter the house because it smells strongly of cats and litter boxes and is filthy. It should be a home like yours or mine – not necessarily immaculate, but not obviously dirty or smelly. The cats may have the run of the house or be kept in their own room, and that too should be warm, clean, and pleasant. Remember: this is their training for coming to your home.

You need not be surprised if a breeder asks you to disinfect your hands before you handle the kittens, for exactly these health reasons. You may have handled your own cat or have visited another breeder before you came to this household, and you may be carrying infection. For this reason it is best not to go from one breeder's house to another if you are looking at several different kittens – choose another day for your next visit, just to make sure you don't bring infection from one litter to another.

You may be taken to an outside shed where the kittens have been bred – this may be absolutely immaculate and so reassure you that they are healthy. That said, it should also prompt a series of questions from you about socialization. One of the first things to ask is where the kittens have been reared. They may be brought into the house for you to see, but could have grown up in a very sterile environment in the outside shed – safe from infection, but failing to learn all those vital lessons in life such as what a vacuum cleaner sounds like, the smell of cooking, that children make loud noises, dogs bark, televisions chatter away in the corner, and that things get dropped, clattered, and banged around the average home. Therefore, it is much better if the kitten has been raised in a home environment. Its first few weeks may have been in one room with its mother, but later on it may have had the run of the house or a selection of rooms at certain periods, perhaps in the evening – it could have a working knowledge of television theme tunes already! A kitten that has seen the blank walls of a shed without having to deal with change or challenge may not be able to do so in its new home and may be nervous or timid. A good breeder will be all too aware of her responsibilities to socialize her kittens and will explain what she has done to ensure this is taken care of properly. If the breeder looks blank at the question or makes excuses, you should be suspicious.

When you actually get to see the kitten, you are being offered the chance to assess its behavior. Give it time to get used to you – a stranger – being there in its house. It may wander up to you and climb all over you. It may be slightly wary of strangers and not necessarily approach you but still carry on confidently with what it is doing – that is fine. What you don't want to see is a terrified kitten that tries to get away and hide from you and is unable to cope with the situation of a new person in its home. If the breeder thinks that you need to give the kitten a bit more time, a basically confident and bold one that is momentarily wary will soon forget to worry and get on with the interesting things in life.

Ask the breeder if you can handle the kitten. Look at it carefully. It should have bright, clear eyes and be interested and alert. It should feel solid and be full of energy. The kitten should not be sneezing or have runny eyes or look at all under the weather. Its ears should be clean and not have any obvious wax or dirt inside. The area under its tail should be clean and dry. The kitten's skin should look healthy and there should be no signs of fleas (or flea feces, which looks like small black specks) or any bald patches or dandruffy areas.

The kitten may be shy at first, as it will not be familiar with you, but a healthy, confident kitten should soon relax and even be playful. Don't just grab the kitten – take time to watch and talk quietly to it or even interact with it by playing with a toy. Give it time. Kittens have short spans of attention, like children, and should soon forget you are there or come and investigate you to see what is going on. If the kitten is fearful and obviously not going to come forward or even ignores you, look elsewhere – a fearful kitten may well turn into a fearful cat. If the breeder says that the kitten has been reared outside and not in a normal home environment, it is very important to check this out, as the kitten may well not be relaxed in this environment.

If you like the look of the kitten but are worried it is nervous, spend a little more quiet time with it and see if it simply needs more time to relax. If not, think about looking elsewhere, unless you are happy to take the risk of owning a more nervous cat.

If the breeder mentions that the kitten has been hand-reared, I would hesitate to take it on. Many such kittens are difficult in that they can be quite aggressive if things do not go the way they want – they have not learned to deal with frustration properly as they would with a cat mother. Although some may be fine, I would be wary.

Ask to see the kitten's mother and the rest of the litter if they are available (some may have gone to new homes already). A confident, people-loving mother will be teaching her kittens by example. The breeder should be happy to show her to you. She should be in good health, although she may be a bit out of condition depending on how many kittens she is feeding and what stage of weaning she is at. The rest of the litter should look well and should be relaxed around people. If any of the others look ill, beware, as infectious diseases can spread quickly through a litter of kittens.

Although the personality of the father of the kittens does seem to have an inheritable effect on the kittens, many breeders do not keep stud cats, and most of the time it is not possible to see the father. Male stud cats are often kept in outside runs because of their tendency to spray strong-smelling urine.

Ask the breeder if the parent cats are free from feline leukemia virus (FeLV) and feline immunodeficiency virus (FIV) – there are tests for both of these diseases and keeping cats clear of them should not be a problem. Ask about breed-related problems such as polycystic kidney disease (PKD) in Persians or Exotic Shorthairs. This is an inherited problem in which cysts form inside the kidney and damage it. The kidneys can be checked using ultrasound to see if the cysts are present and a genetic test is being developed. Ask the breeder if this test was performed for both parents and if so, request the official report for your records.

Check that the kitten has been vaccinated (certainly against feline infectious enteritis and cat flu, although it may also be vaccinated against feline leukemia or chlamydophila), and ask to have the vaccination certificate. You will need this in the future when you have your kitten's booster vaccinations or if you need to put the kitten or cat in a cattery.

Find out whether the kitten has been wormed or treated for fleas, with what, and when – you will need to do this again in the future and you don't want to over- or underdose. Ask what litter the kitten uses so you can, initially at least, use the same one for continuity's sake. Likewise, find out what the kitten is eating, or will be eating (if it is not yet weaned). Again, you want to keep using familiar things initially so that the kitten feels secure and its digestive system is used to the food and is less likely to be upset. You can then change it gradually if you want to.

You do not have to make a decision then and there. You can go away and think about it or go and see other kittens until you feel happy. Let the breeder know your decision as soon as you have decided so that she can take the kitten off the market or let other potential buyers know it is still available. If you do want the kitten, the breeder may ask you to leave a deposit if the kitten is not yet old enough to go to its new home. Ask for a receipt for the deposit with details about your kitten on it. And ask if the deposit is refundable if you change your mind – these are the terms on which the breeder will work and it is best to know all of this up front.

Your kitten may come from the breeder with insurance for a few weeks to cover the transfer period – you may want to consider taking the insurance up after this period has passed. Young cats can get themselves into all sorts of scrapes, so it is well worth considering insurance to cover veterinary costs, the cost of the kitten, etc. – check what the terms of the coverage are.

The breeder may also ask you to agree to neuter the kitten so it is not used for breeding, as she may not feel it is suitable. This is why it is important to explain why you want the kitten at the outset – if you want to show or breed, tell the breeder, as it may affect which kittens you can buy for that purpose. Some breeders are now also neutering kittens before they are rehoused.

When you pick up your kitten, you should also take away with you:

- Registration/transfer slip – required to transfer the kitten to you as owner; the breeder will need to complete her part.
- Vaccination certificate.
- Insurance certificate if the kitten is insured.
- Information on the kitten's diet, litter, etc.

Ask the breeder about dealing with any problems and follow up on the advice. Good breeders will be willing to chat with you if you have a worry or even to take the kitten back if for some unforeseen reason you cannot keep it. Some even insist that you sign an agreement stating that if you have to part with the kitten for any reason they will be the first contact you make. Good breeders care very much what happens to their cats throughout their lives, not just until they go out the door with their new owners.

THE ACCIDENTAL LITTER

In the spring, notices offering kittens free to good homes pop up on bulletin boards everywhere, especially in veterinary offices, and in the pet columns in local papers. Many people mean to have their female cats neutered but don't quite get around to it before the local tom starts to take an interest – he will know she is in season before you do! You should be thinking about neutering your kitten from about four months old (see page 192) to ensure this doesn't happen. However, inevitably, either through neglect or simple absentmindedness, cats do become pregnant, and the next thing the owners know is that there is a litter of kittens in the bedroom closet. Thank goodness that very, very few people these days think of destroying the kittens or drowning them, in the tradition of old-fashioned cat-population control.

In fact, accidental litters can provide some of the best-socialized kittens around. Most are born into the family situation, they are introduced to children and other animals from early on, and are usually in the middle of a busy home – ideal for socialization. While such owners often socialize their kittens without realizing it, they may also be unaware of the health implications of having a litter of kittens. The mother may not be vaccinated or wormed and may also be, by virtue of being free-roaming, at risk of contracting other infectious diseases. The mother may not have had good nutrition during her pregnancy or lactation and so may not be in such good condition as the cat of an experienced and knowledgable breeder. However, mother cats do recover and, if then neutered, will not suffer any long-term harm.

You will be able to take home such a cat – it is likely to be a moggie or even a crossbreed with perhaps one pedigree parent – from about seven weeks onward. Bear in mind that it is not protected in any way, and if you have another cat you may want to keep them apart at least until the kitten has had its first vaccination. You will also need to think about worming – most kittens do need to be wormed because they can get worms via their mother's milk. Discuss all of this with your veterinarian when you go in for your kitten's first vaccination when it is about eight weeks old.

You will still need to look at the kittens and see if they have been socialized – in exactly the same way as for a pedigree kitten. See them with their mother, handle them, and see how they react. Check the kitten for bright eyes, clean ears, and healthy skin; ensure it does not have a runny nose or diarrhea. It may have fleas or ear mites, but this is not the end of the world – these can be dealt with when you visit the veterinarian.

You will probably be able to take the kitten home with you then and there, so make sure you are prepared at home (see Chapter 6) and have something to carry the kitten in. Such kittens tend to be found locally, whereas people who buy pedigree kittens will often travel long distances to find the breed they want.

THE RESCUE KITTEN

As we have seen, about a third of moggie owners get their cats from a rescue organization – these may not just be kittens, but often full-grown cats too. However, rescue organizations in certain areas are often inundated with kittens or cats that are pregnant or have just had litters in the spring and summer.

The term "rescue organization" can mean a host of different things. The large charities that have their own shelters are usually very high quality, the housing is immaculate and well built, and cats are kept in their own units and do not mix with others. These shelters are knowledgable about disease control and have a well-thought-through system for caring for the cats while they are there and in matching kittens to their new owners.

At the other end of the scale are people who collect cats in the name of rescue, packing them into their own homes or overcrowded runs. These cats are often ill and are in the ideal position to pass on their disease to all the other cats there. This situation is very stressful for cats, lowering their ability to fight off disease and making the risks even greater. Often the person is overworked, underfunded, and has no time to deal with the individual cats. He or she may mean well, but the cats are actually suffering more than they might have been out in the world fending for themselves.

In between these two scenarios is a wide range of animal shelters. Size is not an indicator of quality – there are many small rescue organizations that are very well run, deal only with a few cats at a time, provide an excellent service to both the cats and the community, and deserve to be supported.

So how do you tell if a particular rescue organization is a good place to get a kitten? Obviously, they vary greatly. There are large national organizations that run their own rescue centers and may also have volunteers who run them under their name; there are smaller organizations; and there are individual people who have, by one means or another, become involved in rescuing cats. Most of these organizations are charities or are in the process of applying to become charities. Most will rehouse cats. Many will rehabilitate, vaccinate, neuter, and treat cats for fleas, worms, and any illness before they go to a new home. There can be a huge difference in quality, not because people do not mean well or want to help cats, but because it actually takes a great deal of time, money, and information to do rescue properly. Dealing with numbers of animals means that you need to completely understand disease control as well as health and behavioral matters. A few simple things will alert you to whether the people running the rescue facility are in control of it rather than the other way around. When it gets out of control, the cats can become neglected – not on purpose, but because there is just too much to do. Plus, if disease runs through the cats, remedying it can be a problem. There are certain things to look for:

- The establishment should be clean and should not smell.
- Cats should be housed individually, or in groups if they came in as such.
- The proprietor should be knowledgable and organized.

- The cats should look relaxed and healthy (bearing in mind some will be recovering from injury or maltreatment).

There are many, many good shelters that do a fantastic job in difficult circumstances; the aim of this discussion is to make you aware of the bad ones where cats may come out worse off than when they went in. These are usually dirty establishments where cats are kept all together in rooms or runs and the cats themselves seem stressed and unwell.

From this kind of establishment, you have a strong chance of getting a kitten that is ill or has not been socialized. The kitten's background may not be known, and the proprietor may simply want to get rid of it without actually finding out what you want and matching your requirements to an appropriate cat.

Of course, all cat lovers will want these poor cats to find homes and may feel it is rather uncharitable of me to suggest that people avoid them. What is important is that you know what you are getting yourself into. Most people want a healthy kitten that is socialized enough to fit into their lives without stress. They may have children who will be very upset if the kitten is ill or even dies. They will feel very distressed if the kitten is terrified of life and tries to avoid everyone and everything in the house. They will feel that they cannot take the kitten back and are basically stuck with it. It is such a shame when a loving family cannot enjoy a happy cat and regrets the decision to get one – it may even prevent them from taking another in the future.

You may be willing to take on an ill kitten and to help it to recuperate – that is fantastic as long as you go in with your eyes (and probably your wallet) open, aware of the problems and the possible heartaches. If it all works out, the rewards are great, but not everybody is willing to do this.

If you want a kitten that is not likely to be ill and which will be confident in your home, don't go to a bad establishment to get one. If you do go and then realize it is not really the best source of a kitten, don't take a kitten because you feel sorry for it, because it is cowering in the corner or looks ill. There is an almost overwhelming desire to help these little creatures and to rescue them from their plight. Remember what you took into consideration when you looked at what you wanted from your cat – an unsocialized, ill cat may never be that cat.

Be careful too if the organization says the kittens are from a feral background. You may be told convincingly that the animals will become more friendly and that they are just scared at the moment. Again, be aware that the kittens may not have been socialized early enough and the confident, interactive cat you want is not actually inside those cats at all – they are simply wild creatures.

Whatever kitten you look at and handle, ask about its background and how much handling it has had. It will probably not have had the chance to see and hear the sights and sounds of a normal home because for the sake of its health and safety it is being housed in a cat unit and run. It may, however, see lots of people going in and out and hear people chatting to one another. Good rescue leagues now try to socialize their kittens better as they are aware of the importance.

Ask about vaccinations and whether the kitten is already neutered. Some rescue organizations now neuter kittens before they are rehoused in case new owners forget to neuter them or just don't get around to it in time and the whole cycle starts again. Kittens can be neutered at quite a young age without any adverse effects. They may also be partially or fully vaccinated when you get them. A great deal of money may already have been spent on the kitten, so do not shirk if you are asked for a donation for it to enable the charity to help more cats.

6

Preparing at Home

Having decided on your kitten, or kittens, and perhaps even chosen it, you need to prepare. It's like bringing a new baby home from the hospital – the anticipation is lovely. Kittens don't need very much in the way of equipment, but there are some things that are essential and others that can make life easier or more comfortable.

You will obviously have to feed the kitten and provide somewhere for it to go to the bathroom. It will need a bed, and you will need something to bring it home in. These are the first and most vital requirements. Other things such as toys and scratch posts can be bought a little bit later. You will also need to give some thought to where the kitten is going to sleep and eat and where its litter box should be situated.

FEEDING UTENSILS AND FOOD

Visit any pet shop or superstore and you will find an array of bowls made from plastic, stainless steel, or ceramic. Choose a bowl the appropriate size for your kitten so that it can get to the food or water but cannot wade into it (kittens often climb onto a saucer to eat). It helps if the bowl has a nonslip base so that it does not travel across the floor as the kitten tries to eat. Choose something that is easy to wash. Some people say that plastic bowls retain the smell of food, in which case it might be better to choose stainless steel or ceramic – plastic does become scratched after a period of use too. Keep the bowls clean and always ensure the kitten has a supply of fresh, clean water.

Initially, even if only for the first couple of days, try to use the same food that the breeder or previous owner fed to the kitten. Kittens can get upset tummies very easily – a change of diet at a time when everything else is also new may just trigger a bout of diarrhea. It is also nice for the kitten to find something with which it is familiar; smells are very important in this context. Familiar food will be comforting.

You may feel that the kitten's diet is not correct or that you prefer to use a different brand of food – make the changes carefully and gradually. Your kitten should be on a special kitten diet, formulated to take into account its rapid growth. It needs all the nutrients for building muscle as well as energy for play and learning. There are many such good kitten diets on the market to choose from. You may decide on a wet food, one that comes in a can or pouch, or a dry diet that is easy to use. Check how much you should be feeding and how often. Kittens, like babies, need food often and in small amounts – they have small stomachs but lots of energy and need frequent refueling. If you are feeding a dry diet, you can simply leave it out for the kitten to eat as it wants. A wet diet may go stale if left in the dish, may not smell nice, or may attract flies in the summer. Wet food needs to be thrown away if it is not eaten, and the dish should be washed thoroughly.

Some people decide they want to feed a home-prepared diet – this can be very tricky in terms of providing all the nutrients a growing kitten needs. A chicken breast may be appealing to us, but it does not have all the nutrients that are required – the normal diet of a free-living kitten consists of small mammals or birds, and they will eat all parts of the body in order to get the balance of energy, minerals, and vitamins they need. Cat nutrition is a complex science, and you would need to feed a wide range of meat and fish, supplemented with all the necessary vitamins and minerals. Moreover, the results can be haphazard, especially at a time when your kitten's body is demanding very specific nutrients for healthy growth and development. Unless you know what you are doing, it is safer, and generally easier, to use a commercially prepared kitten food. The pet food companies spend millions on getting it right and making it easy for us.

Don't even consider using a vegetarian diet for your kitten. Cats have evolved to become highly efficient hunters, and, because of their success in feeding themselves on prey, they have not needed to rely on vegetable matter as a source of nutrition. Their bodies have adapted by losing some of the chemical pathways needed to deal with a vegetarian diet. They have nutritional requirements that can only be satisfied by eating meat, for which reason we call the cat an obligate carnivore – without meat in its diet, it can suffer from diseases related to deficiencies in certain proteins and fats. Like humans and most mammals, cats use protein in food to build body tissue and carry out repairs and also to build things such as hormones. Cats also use protein in the way we use carbohydrate, as a source of energy. So the type, quality, and proportion of protein in their diets are very important. Some vegetarian diets now claim to have found nonanimal sources for all of these nutrients, but to me the whole thing is nonsense. The cat looks and acts as it does because millions of years of evolution have made it into a hunter – we should respect and accept this and not try to make it into a rabbit.

Look at the way a free-living or feral cat will eat. It will spend a great deal of time hunting; many hunts will not be successful, but it will need ten or more small meals a day to keep it going, depending on just how active it is. The cat is a snacker rather than a huge meal eater. You will notice that if you provide dry food for your cat, it will have a few mouthfuls and then wander off and do something else, then come back and take some more. If there is nothing in the bowl, the cat will soon start to nag you to put some in there. If you feed it wet or canned food, remember this can go bad quickly, especially in warm weather (or in warm heated houses) and will not be palatable to the cat, which has a very sensitive nose for these things.

A kitten needs small, frequent meals in order to be able to ingest enough nutrients to provide the energy and building blocks for rapid growth. It therefore needs to be fed more frequently than an adult cat. When you first get your kitten at about eight to twelve weeks of age, it will need about five meals a day. If you choose to feed dry food, your life will be easier when you go out, as the kitten can help itself. If you want to use canned food, you might want to invest in an automatic feeder, which will pop open at a pre-set time and give the kitten access to fresh food. Feeding provides an opportunity to bond with your kitten, so enjoy these interactions and make the most of them in terms of interactions. By the time your kitten is six months old it will be about three-quarters grown and you can reduce meal times to twice a day if you wish or continue to feed dry food on a free-choice basis.

When you are preparing your home for your kitten's arrival, you will need to think about where you are going to feed. Find a quiet spot where there is no competition from other cats or where the dog is not likely to swoop down and polish off the bowl in one mouthful (cat food is very, very appealing to dogs!). Also make sure the food is served away from the litter box.

Milk has always been thought of as the traditional drink for cats. However, cats and weaned kittens do not require milk as part of their diet and it is not a substitute for water. After a kitten is weaned, its ability to digest lactose, a sugar found in milk, is lost. If it is then given milk it cannot digest it properly, which can result in diarrhea. Check with the breeder or place where you got the kitten as to whether it has had milk before and if it was tolerated. There are now special milks made for cats that do not cause stomach upset, so you may want to try one of these. However, do not start this until the kitten has settled in – too much change and new additions to the diet are best avoided at the beginning.

LITTER AND LITTER BOXES

Even if you ultimately intend your kitten to go outside and use the yard as its toilet, you will need to keep it in until it has had its vaccinations, or to at least bond it to your home (if it is fully vaccinated already). Whatever the reason, you will need a litter box either permanently or for a few months at least. There will also be other times when the cat is ill or when you want to keep it indoors and you will need a litter box on hand, so it is worth getting one that will be large enough and durable enough to use when the cat is older. Litter boxes come in a wide range of sizes and styles, from the large, simple open tray type to the sophisticated one that sifts and removes waste. In the changeover from the previous owner to your home, you may want to use something that the kitten is familiar with – even if only in choosing an open type or one with a lid – so that the kitten recognizes it and knows what to do. Later on you may want to change this if you find something you or your cat prefer. It is helpful to use a box with high sides so that the kitten does not scrape the litter all over the floor, but make sure it is not too high to actually climb into. It should be big enough for your kitten to turn around in as it scratches at the litter.

When choosing which type of litter to use, again, try to begin at least with something the kitten is familiar with. Thereafter you can gradually change to another litter or soil from the yard if you want your kitten to start using the yard (but wait until all vaccinations are complete before doing this). There are many and various types of litter, from the traditional fuller's earth clay-based form to wood- and paper-based pellets to more organic types and fine-grain sandy litters. What you choose may depend on its weight (if you have to carry it home from the shop) or its texture (if it tracks around the house on the kitten's feet because it is fine). If you have a long-haired kitten, this may influence your choice, as some litter may stick to the kitten's coat around its tail and back legs.

Some litters come with built-in deodorizing chemicals, air fresheners, or perfumes to help cover up or reduce smells coming from the box. These odors can be quite strong to the human sense of smell, let alone that of cats, some of which may not like the strength of the scent. It is much better to clean the box more frequently than to try and mask the smell. Likewise, some cats do not like standing on pellets while others are quite happy to use them. See how your kitten reacts. Cats usually prefer the finer-grained sand-like litters, but these do tend to stick to their feet a bit. Put a dirt-collecting mat under the box to catch the fine grains before they get walked around the house.

Using newspaper in the litter box may be a cheap option, but it is not particularly absorbent – the kitten cannot dig in it the same way, and the ink may come off on the kitten's feet. The kitten may also come to associate newspaper with its toilet and use paper that is lying around the house after being read (or even before!).

When you first bring your kitten home you will want to confine it to a room or even use a special pen or dog crate when you are out. You will want to position the box where the kitten can find it easily, but in a quiet position, not out in the open, where the kitten can feel safe. Depending on the space you have available, do not place it too near its bed or food, as kittens are taught by their mothers to move away from the nest area to go to the bathroom.

If you have a dog or a toddler in the house, make sure it cannot get to the litter box – either to eat or play with the contents, or to grab or annoy the kitten as it uses the box, which may deter the cat from using it in the first place. If you have another cat, do not assume the kitten is going to use the same litter box. Indeed, until the kitten has had its full vaccination course, this is not a good idea. If you follow the suggestions for introductions, the kitten and resident cat will not meet up initially anyway, so a separate box is the best idea. The kitten must be able to get to the box 24 hours a day.

Think about how you are going to disinfect the litter box so that you have the correct products in the house. You will need to empty it daily and wash it with hot water and soap. It is the disinfectant you need to be careful with. Disinfectants are made to be lethal to some viruses, bacteria, or fungi, and they can be dangerous to other organisms, depending on how they work. Some common disinfectants can be very dangerous for cats. Cleaning products that contain phenols can be toxic to cats; a rough rule of thumb is to avoid disinfectants that turn cloudy when you put them in water. Cats are also very sensitive to cresols and chloroxylenols found in other disinfectants. Other chemicals to steer clear of include hexachlorophone, iodine, and iodophos. If you are worried, check the disinfectant container for details or ask your veterinarian. Disinfectants that are made for use in kennels and catteries or veterinary clinics are safe for cats. However, a good standby is bleach, diluted as suggested on the product. Rinse out the litter box after disinfection. Whatever disinfectant you choose for the litter box, do not be tempted to use a higher strength or dilute it less than is recommended on the label because you think this will kill more bugs – making the disinfectant more concentrated can increase the danger of a low-toxicity product.

A BED

Kittens love to be cozy. Just like kids who will make a den or surround themselves with their cuddly toys, pillows, or blankets, kittens enjoy the warmth and the safe feeling of being surrounded and snug – womb-like, you might say. A bed for a kitten can range from something as simple as a small cardboard box with a warm blanket or cushion inside to a customized bed. There are lots to choose from, many with hoods or igloo-type styles that protect the kitten all the way around as well as keeping out drafts and noise. Kittens love all of the synthetic furs and fleeces that they can snuggle up in and that are, thankfully, very easy to wash and quick to dry – ideal for babies. Think safety – be wary of using bean bags that might have holes where those small polystyrene balls can escape, wicker baskets that might get chewed, or knitted fabrics that can get caught up on small claws. Cats tend to love the hammock-style beds that hang on radiators – not only are they warm and snuggly, but they lift the kitten up so it can see what is going on in the household. Over time and as it gets the run of the whole house, your kitten may choose its own favorite napping and sleeping places, but at the beginning when it is more confined you need to provide something it will like.

A CRATE OR PEN

One of the most useful things you can have if you have a new kitten, or kittens, is a special pen, dog crate, or indoor kennel. These are available from pet shops, or you may even be able to borrow one – they collapse down when you are not using them. They are always useful to have at a later date if you are introducing new animals to the household or if your cat needs to be confined because it is ill or injured. These are also recommended when people take on a new puppy, as they are excellent for safety, to help with toilet training, and to give the pup a place it recognizes as its den.

In the first few weeks after you bring your kitten home, a crate is a great asset. If you have other animals it makes introductions simpler and safer. It will also enable you to confine the kitten when you are not watching it and know that it is safe. Kittens get into all sorts of mischief and into all types of small spaces; they will sample electric wires or escape from open windows if they get bored or just because they are very inquisitive. Putting them in the pen at night and when you are out of the house means you can relax about their safety. For the kitten, it is a den that it is familiar with and feels secure inside.

The crate should be large enough to allow your kitten to move around inside and to be able to accommodate a bed, a litter box, and a bowl of water or food. You can line the bottom with newspaper to catch any spills from the litter box or if the water bowl gets turned over. You can also put a blanket or cover over it if you want the kitten to feel more secure or just to quiet it down. Kittens take to them very well and are quite happy when inside. You can let the kitten out to venture into certain rooms or the whole house, but it will know where to come back to find its bed and litter box, and you will often find the kitten has gone back inside for a nap.

Deciding where to place the pen may simply depend on where you have space. A large kitchen can be ideal. It gives you quick access to water, food, and cleaning equipment and is usually nice and warm. It is the center of the home. People come and go, and there is usually lots of activity for the kitten to watch; it gives it the chance to get used to the comings and goings within the house and to those who live and visit there. It allows for safe meetings with other pets and lets them get used to one another. The dining or living room is also a good site. You may want to have the kitten in a quiet place initially, but it should be able to experience the family and your lifestyle after a week or so, depending on whether you have other animals you want to introduce (see page 121).

TOYS

If you don't have time to shop for toys for your kitten, the old standbys of small balls of rolled-up paper and pieces of string will be just fine. These do require some effort from you but will give you the chance to interact and play with your kitten (see Chapter 11). If you are buying toys, make sure they are safe (for example, ensure that the eyes, ears, whiskers, feathers, or other attachments won't fall off and be swallowed).

SCRATCH POST

A scratch post functions not just for claw maintenance but can also be a great source of amusement for kittens. Many come as part of cat exercise centers with platforms and posts, places to hide and sleep. Kittens love these and will rush up and down them with great enthusiasm. It is good to get kittens using a scratch post early on so that they want to keep using it rather than the living room furniture or the carpet! Scratching has several important functions. It removes the outer layer of the claw to reveal a sharp new point underneath, and it also allows the cat to deposit scent from glands between the pads on the underside of the paws. While kittens will not yet be interested in spreading scents, they soon will be aware of the need to do this and of places that have been anointed – if the scratch post is already such a signpost they will continue to use it. This is one of the cat's natural behaviors that it needs to be able to enact. A great deal of scratching is done outdoors, which is fine and only damages fence posts or tree bark – indoors it can cause stress if the wallpaper or furniture is being destroyed. Many people declaw the front paws of their cats to prevent furniture damage. Many others see this as a painful, unnecessary procedure, and some veterinarians will not undertake the operation. More and more cat-lovers are coming around to this way of thinking.

Scratch posts come in a variety of types, from wooden branches to sisal-wrapped posts. Choose one that allows the kitten (and remember it will rapidly grow a lot more) to stretch up and pull down, giving it a really good pull on its claws. Also make sure that it is stable and doesn't topple on the kitten.

GROOMING EQUIPMENT

If you are getting a short-haired kitten, then grooming equipment will not be high on your shopping list. Your kitten will probably enjoy being groomed with a soft brush – an old toothbrush will be fine initially – even if it doesn't actually need it. Long-haired cats such as Persians are a different matter, and you can never start grooming too early. Getting them used to being brushed and combed, having their eyes wiped and their coat tidied up, and being trimmed under the tail is essential if you want them to enjoy or even just tolerate this procedure when they are older. Dealing with a cat that doesn't want to be groomed becomes more and more stressful. The more it fights, the longer you put off the grooming and the more knots and mats form in the coat. You don't want it to be a battle, so making it into an enjoyable procedure early on is essential. Start with a soft brush and a wide-toothed comb, and talk to the breeder about what he or she has found most useful for that particular coat type – there are all sorts of tips and hints that can help enormously. A fine-toothed comb like a flea comb may also be useful. If you need to cut out a tangle, use a pair of scissors with blunt or rounded ends – if the kitten fidgets while you are snipping you will not stab it with sharp ends. See page 132 for tips on grooming and cleaning.

SAFETY FIRST

Consider your kitten as a toddler that can scale a mountain or jump over almost any obstacle put in front of it, squeeze into a tiny hole in the floor, or crawl under the piano. It may have different motivations for wanting to do these things, but they all have the potential to end in tears!

If you have a very confident kitten, it will probably be very nosy and will try to do things a more sensible, older cat would decide were just too dangerous. The saying "curiosity killed the cat" is probably based on truth. Kittens do want to sniff things and poke them with their paws or even chew them to have a taste; they are interested in moving machines and warm clothes driers. They want to find out what is on top of the cabinet or out of the window. And while they have inherent climbing skills, they may not have honed them precisely enough for the feat of balance required.

If you are bringing home a kitten that seemed nervous at its previous home, be prepared for it to be even more nervous when you place it in an entirely foreign environment with no visual or smell cues with which to associate. Its first impulse will be to hide, and quickly. It is likely to dash for a dark place where it can feel safe. This may be under the bed or sofa, up the chimney, or in a small space under the bathtub. This is a distinct probability, as anyone who has handled nervous or feral kittens will tell you – they will always find somewhere you have not thought of.

Therefore, it is essential to try to make your home safe for your new kitten – to protect it from itself as much as anything else. Imagine that you are small but very agile. Get down on the floor and look at things from that small-kitten perspective – things will look very different, and you may notice small holes or potential hazards that were not obvious from the vantage point of five to six feet up – human adult eye level. You may want to choose a room for the kitten initially that you know is safe and has no such possibilities.

If you have a number of people in the house, it might be time for a family conference. Get the children to imagine they are small kittens and do a tour of the house, noting the dangers. This may be a good way to help them remember that they need to keep doors and windows shut, as well as the clothes drier and washing machine. They need to know to take action if the kitten climbs up near the stovetop when it is on – children are actually very good at imagining a host of scary scenarios. Likewise, burning candles can be fascinating and the fireplace may need some protection until the kitten realizes what they are. Electric cords that are hanging loose may entice a chew, and small items such as elastic bands may get swallowed. If you sew, a round-up of pins and needles that have evaded the pincushion or sewing kit would be a good idea. Pieces of thread can also get caught in teeth or around the kitten's tongue. If you do have a cord chewer, a routine of unplugging appliances before the kitten is left in a particular room would be a good idea.

Some active kittens do indeed climb the curtains, so be prepared for this to happen. Those kittens that undertake this exciting exercise usually keep it up until they are too heavy to do it easily – or until the curtains fall down! You may just have to accept it, ignore any damage, and hope the phase passes quickly. Although cats have a reputation for falling on their feet, they can be injured by falls – plummeting to the tiled kitchen floor from the top of the plate rack can cause injury. If this happens, keep a careful eye on the kitten and take it to the veterinarian if it seems injured or is acting strangely.

Kittens like to chew on plants – outdoors, cats would nibble grass or herbs. However, if they are indoors and there is no grass available, or even simply because they are curious, they may nibble at other plants or even flowers in vases. There are some plants that are very toxic to cats and even a small bite might be extremely dangerous for a small kitten, which would only need a small dose of poison to cause problems. Some common houseplants such as dumb cane and umbrella plants are poisonous, as are many flowers commonly used in bouquets. These include cornflowers, delphiniums, hyacinths, monkshood, and many members of the lily family. The Feline Advisory Bureau has a list of poisonous plants on its web site (www.fabcats.org) so you can check out those you have at home and especially those the kitten will have access to.

Most cats do not eat poisonous plants when they have access to the garden. However, a kitten may decide to play with something like the seeds from a laburnum tree, which are poisonous. It pays to be aware of what you have in the yard because kittens are rather impetuous. If you have small children, you will probably have thought through a lot of these things already.

And just as you need to keep family medicines and cleaning materials away from small children, do the same for your kitten – bearing in mind that it can climb or jump onto surfaces that keep things safely out of reach of toddlers. Some human medicines such as aspirin are toxic to cats and should not be left where they can be sampled. Never be tempted to medicate your kitten yourself – human or dog medicines can be fatal to kittens because they need very small doses. Other substances such as onion powder, cocoa, and excesses of fish oils or liver can also be poisonous.

OTHER SMALL CREATURES

If you already own a caged bird, such as a parrot or canary, or a small mammal, such as a mouse or hamster, you need to take care of them when the kitten is around. Their movements will be highly attractive to a kitten. Letting them out of the cage while the kitten is around is obviously not a good idea, but you also need to ensure the cage is kitten-proof and that it cannot be knocked off a shelf or hook and crash to the floor. I would never trust a kitten with another small creature – while it may not intend to eat it (although it may well try), it can do a lot of physical damage if it gets hold of it, and the fear may kill the bird or mammal without obvious injury.

TRAVELING HOME

You could bring the kitten home in a cardboard box, but, as you are likely to need a carrier through the cat's life for trips to the veterinarian or the cattery, it is worth getting one from the very start, when picking the kitten up. There are lots of carriers available for you to choose from; their materials range from cardboard to plastic and wicker. Cardboard may be fine for a short emergency, but it is not strong and will go soggy if the cat urinates in the box, which it is quite likely to do. Plastic flat-pack ones are fine for an emergency but will have only a short life. It is better to invest in a sturdy carrier right from the start. You need something that is strong, easily washed, and simple to open and shut so that you can get the cat in and out smoothly. Front-opening wicker baskets look very pretty, but trying to extract a frightened cat through the small front entrance when it has its feet secured in the wicker walls and jammed against the door surround is not much fun. It is also difficult to clean. Choose something that opens at the top, or at the top and side, so you can easily get to a frightened cat and lift it out rather than trying to pull it out. Lift the carrier without the cat in it and see how heavy it is. If you are using one that you have had for many years for previous cats, make sure the lid fits properly, as kittens can squeeze through small spaces.

When you pick up the kitten, line the carrier with something absorbent such as newspaper, or bedding material that is warm and cozy but easily washable. Ask the owner or breeder not to feed the kitten just before you travel or to give it only a small amount of food. If you are picking up a pedigree kitten, remember to get all of the paperwork outlined in Chapter 5.

Pop the kitten in the carrier and either strap it into the car with the seatbelt (to avoid catapulting it across the car if you have to brake sharply), put it safely into the footwell behind a seat, or set it in the back if you have a sport utility vehicle. Do not put it into the trunk. Place something waterproof under the carrier in case of large accidents that are not entirely absorbed by the lining of the carrier. If you are traveling a long distance, take some baby wipes or old towels in case you have to clean up the kitten – a frightened kitten may urinate or defecate and get itself in a mess. Most kittens will never have been outside the house where they were born, so this could be a rather frightening experience. The kitten may cry or meow on the way to your home. Try not to worry – if it is warm and secure, it can come to no harm. Talk to it quietly and concentrate on getting home safely. The kitten may feel more secure if you place a blanket over the carrier to darken the interior. However, if it is a very hot day make sure there is plenty of ventilation so that the kitten does not overheat. If the weather is at all warm do not leave the kitten in the car while you have a coffee to break the journey – temperatures in vehicles can rise very, very quickly and kittens are very vulnerable to heatstroke. Take a thermos and keep the windows open when you stop to make sure the car is kept cool. It goes without saying that if you open the kitten's carrier make sure all windows and doors are shut. If you are traveling for a couple of hours, you will need to offer the kitten the use of a litter box and some water during the journey.

Now that the house is ready and the kitten is home – how can you best help it to settle in?

7

Settling Your Kitten In

It's very exciting to take your new kitten home for the first time – like bringing a new baby back from the hospital. Everyone is waiting to see the new arrival and cuddle it. If you have a household with children, it is worth explaining to them that everything will be very strange for the kitten and it will be nervous (even if it is quite a bold kitten). Try to hold everyone back from rushing to cuddle it or play with it.

Everything will be new – the sights, sounds, voices, smells, the behaviors of the strange humans, and even different animals. So anything familiar will help the kitten to settle in – food and litter it knows and, if possible, a scent from its old home. When you leave the breeder or previous owner or shelter, see if you can bring a small bit of its bedding with you, just to tide the kitten over until it gets used to the new smells. It's a bit like a security blanket that many children use to help them get to sleep or to clutch for reassurance when they are a bit nervous. Scent is hugely important to cats – equivalent to humans' excellent sight. Cats rely heavily on smells to understand what is going on around them.

Choose a room for the kitten to settle into initially – it doesn't need access to the whole house, it just needs to gain confidence with the familiarity of one room. If you are using a kitten pen or crate, you have more chance of controlling the kitten's activities. Give the kitten a small portion of food, water, a litter box, and a cozy bed (with its familiar bedding if you have any). Give food sparingly and often if the kitten seems to tolerate it well – stress can cause tummy upsets, so giving the digestive tract time to deal with a little bit at a time is better than having to cope with a huge meal. This is especially important if you are giving the kitten food it is not familiar with. Lift the kitten onto the litter box every so often so that it realizes that the litter is there and what it is for – it may be so intent in watching all the new things around it that it forgets to relieve itself.

Much as it is very tempting to cuddle and coo over the kitten, let it rest from the journey, eat something, and use the litter box. It may have a snooze because kittens, like small children, need a lot of rest. If the kitten seems very relaxed and happy to be with you, you might hold it while it is asleep, sitting quietly so that it can rest. However, it might be quite nervous and want to cuddle down in its bed and watch what is going on while still feeling safe. Even confident, well-socialized kittens used to the goings-on in one particular household may be nervous and retiring for a while. Give them a chance to find their feet. If you have chosen a kitten that seems outgoing and confident, it will adapt quite quickly. Of course, kittens vary in the way they respond to their first night away from their old home. Some may saunter around, take over the dog's bed, and generally boss everyone about; others need some time to acclimatize to unfamiliar surroundings. Then you can start to introduce new people or animals in a controlled manner (as I will discuss later).

Talk in a quiet, reassuring voice and allow the kitten to investigate new objects and smells at its own pace – the smaller the area to be explored, the braver it is likely to be.

Don't panic if the kitten squeezes under the sofa or coffee-table. The worst thing you can do is to chase it around and drag it out from somewhere it may only be hiding temporarily or just exploring. Lure the kitten out by pulling along a piece of string and calling for food. Provided you have ensured that all escape routes and small, dangerous holes are blocked off, you know the kitten is safe in the room. Give it a little time. If you have taken on a very nervous kitten that decides it is not coming out for anything, you need to choose a room for it that is safe – the best thing to use for this is, again, a kitten pen or crate. The kitten can curl up in a covered bed and feel safe, while still being able to gradually become familiar with the household and its occupants and routines. It is kept safe but can still learn that none of the things happening around it will harm it. You can also check up on the kitten regularly instead of having to hunt around the house for its latest hiding place.

LITTER TRAINING

Most kittens come already litter trained by their mothers, and, even if they are not, they are fast learners. Kittens will automatically paw at loose, soil-like substances, so half the battle is already fought. When you first arrive home with the kitten put it into the litter box so it has a chance to relieve itself. If nothing happens, try again at regular intervals. Gently move the kitten's paws to rake at the litter so that it gets the idea. Kittens often want to go to the toilet after they wake up and after they eat – use these times to the best advantage. If the kitten has an accident outside the box, mop up the offending solids or liquids, put them onto the litter, and place the kitten into the box again. You are aiming to help the kitten to associate the litter box with the functions you wish it to perform there.

It is also important to clean the area of the accident carefully with something like a biological washing powder so that the smell is removed as well as possible and the kitten is not attracted back there to use it again. Never punish the kitten for accidents – this will not teach it anything and will only function to make the kitten fearful of you. Always encourage the behavior you want and put effort into trying to ensure that accidents don't happen.

You may need to remind the kitten where the box is over the first few days, particularly if it has free access to quite a large area – anyone who has potty-trained a toddler knows that they can get so engrossed in what they are doing that they don't get to the potty in time. This is another good reason to limit the kitten's access to the whole house at first or to return it to its pen or den room regularly.

HANDLING YOUR KITTEN

Think about how we like to cuddle our cats and pick them up. Cats that do not live with people would never be in a situation where they are lifted off the ground and made so very vulnerable in this way. Holding cats can be alarming and very stressful for them. A cat's natural reaction to any threat is to try to get away from the situation fast. Therefore, it doesn't like to get itself into a situation where its escape is prohibited. Holding cats is restraining them, and they have to learn that this is not threatening and that they are not in danger. Thus, handling, stroking, and picking up are all important lessons of kittenhood. We also have to make sure that we get it right.

Some kittens are happy to be handled and enjoy being stroked and picked up. This depends both on their genetic makeup and how used they are to handling. Like small children, their attention span may be quite short, and while they will tolerate some handling, they will wriggle to get away and do something else, not enjoying too much confinement. Others may enjoy playing but do not like to be handled. Still others may not be people-oriented at all and may let you know that they are very unhappy about being picked up, and with close contact in general. Whichever type of kitten you have, forcing the issue is not going to work. Slow and gentle encouragement may eventually work, depending on the kitten's background – you can only try! Confidence is very important, so the way you approach and hold the kitten will influence how it looks forward to or avoids such attention in the future. Always be firm, gentle, and confident about your approach. Pick up your kitten by scooping it up under the chest area with one hand while supporting its hindquarters with the other. Carry the kitten by keeping your hand under its chest with your fingers between its front legs, then close your arm into your side so that the kitten's weight is supported by your body. Your other hand will then be free to hold its head, stroke it encouragingly, or even hold it by the scruff of the neck in an emergency.

Some kittens enjoy being on their owners so much that they climb up their legs or jump on them as they pass. This is very flattering and quite amusing, but usually quite painful, especially when the kitten gets heavier and its claws become sharper – it can also ruin clothes pretty successfully. Some kittens enjoy traveling

about on their owners' shoulders – no problem if you are happy with this. If you do not want your kitten to leap on you as you pass, you will need to lift it off quickly, walk away, and not give it any attention at all – this is what it is after. If it does not succeed this way but gets lots of attention when it approaches you gently on the floor or when you are sitting down, it will soon choose what type of action to take.

MAKING INTRODUCTIONS

If it is just you or you and your partner who inhabit the kitten's new home, you can take introductions slowly and gently. If you have children (especially young ones) and other pets, you need to take the time to make introductions carefully, laying down the ground rules for the children and making sure that other pets are safe to be around. A kitten that has already met small people, with their high voices and tendency to become excited and rather loud, will take new ones much more in stride than a kitten that has only met, for example, an adult woman. Likewise, a kitten used to dogs will adapt to a new one much more easily than one that has not met canines at all. And then there may be the resident cat – probably the most difficult problem of all. Don't assume that your animals will welcome the new arrival with open arms – dogs may be too enthusiastic and cats are more likely to be totally unenthusiastic! Stay calm and don't expect it all to be rosy immediately.

INTRODUCING CHILDREN

Even people who do not have children can find them a rather alien species, so kittens too, even if they are used to adults, may need time to get used to smaller humans that walk, talk, and probably smell different than adults. If you have children, avoid getting a nervous kitten. Opt for a confident, responsive, and inquisitive one, and life will be much more pleasant for people and cat alike.

Taking the time to explain to the children that the kitten is not a toy, that it is very vulnerable, and that it is likely to be scared of them at first should help them to approach it in the right way. Giving them the responsibility of trying to be kind and quiet with it will encourage them. Don't wait until the child has grabbed the kitten and then shout at it for doing it wrong, scaring the kitten and the child half to death. Lead by example and teach the children how to hold the kitten properly. Explain that sudden movements and loud voices may make the kitten panic. Get the kids to sit on the floor and let the kitten walk around and onto them. Letting the children offer a small food treat will also help to show them where the kitten may like to be stroked, on its head and along its back – no tail pulling, though! Explain the basics of feline body language (you may have to do some homework on this yourself or give the kids the task of telling you about it, depending on their age). Point out the warning signs of a stressed or frightened kitten – flattened ears, struggling to get away, swishing tail, hissing, etc. –

and emphasize that any of these really do mean that the children must back off. Also make sure they know that the kitten may be upset and reactive for some time afterward and to let it settle down and approach it in a different way in the future.

Discourage grabbing and squeezing – kittens are quite fragile and hard squeezing could be painful and frightening and put them off being picked up entirely. They may even scratch the child, who may then drop the kitten! Instruct the children to let the kitten walk away, no matter how desperate they are to play with it. The novelty will wear off quite soon, but at the beginning young children may be very intense about handling the kitten. Prevent chasing and disturbing the kitten if it is resting. Younger children should never be left alone with a kitten, as kittens are very fragile and easily injured; bad handling can permanently put them off being picked up or cuddled. Larger kittens can also scratch quite badly if driven to it, so there are health aspects to consider on both sides.

If the groundwork is handled carefully, kittens and children can make great pals. Having a pet is a great introduction to responsibility and caring for another creature, thereby growing the cat lovers of the future. And in turn, cats make great confidants and companions.

Bringing a new cat or kitten into your home and introducing it to your resident cat or dog can be quite nerve racking. You want them all to get along together and welcome the new feline into the house, but this seldom happens quite so easily – even though your reason for getting another cat may be to keep your resident cat company, it may not rush out and welcome the newcomer with open paws! Careful introductions can help smooth the way toward the harmonious merging of animals. Controlling the situation rather than leaving the animals to sort it out for themselves will promote a smooth meeting and the best possible start together.

Remember too that kittens have periods of intense activity and then need lots of sleep. Too much handling can overexhaust a kitten, and it may sleep instead of eating. Give kittens time and space to eat and rest.

INTRODUCING THE DOG

Traditionally we have represented cats and dogs as natural enemies – probably the result of watching too many cartoons on TV. While cats and dogs may be wary of each other initially, they do not see the other as direct competition and can actually get along very well. And while some breeds of dogs will enjoy chasing strange cats, most dogs and cats are very good company for each other and even seem to be quite affectionate. Some choose to sleep in the same bed or in a pile together in front of the fire, or even to play friendly chase games. This kind of relationship is usually the result of good early experience and socialization for both species, but it can also be achieved by careful and patient introductions.

If you are unsure as to how your dog will react to a new kitten, you need to proceed carefully. If the dog has lived with cats before, it may show interest initially in the new recruit to the household, but after that it will settle back into doing what it is told by the latest cat! Introducing them using a cage or with the dog on a collar and leash until its early enthusiasm and curiosity pass will usually be enough. The dog will soon settle down, the novelty will wear off, and it will begin to see the new cat as part of the pack. Many dogs will live happily with their own cats while chasing strange felines out of the yard, so you will need to take care until the cat is seen as one of the household. Likewise, if your new cat or kitten has previously lived with a dog, it will be much less likely to be frightened for long and will become confident around the dog more quickly.

However, safety must come first initially. You will need to keep everything under control until the dog and cat have grown used to each other. Stroke the dog and cat separately but without washing your hands to exchange their scents. The cat will then take on the smell profile of the house and become part of the dog's pack. Once again, the large pen is ideal for first meetings to keep the situation calm and the cat protected. Let the dog sniff the newcomer through the bars and get over its initial excitement. The cat may well hiss and spit, but it is well protected. If you have a large pen, then you can put the cat in this at night in the room where the dog sleeps and let them get used to each other for a few days or even a week, depending on how used to cats the dog is.

If you have a dog that has not met a cat before, you need to take more care. Consider the breed of dog you have – some breeds, like greyhounds, are natural chasers; others naturally worry and chase – for example, terriers. Do you know your dog's background? If you have a dog from an animal shelter, you may not know if it has a history of liking or actively disliking cats, so you just need to take things slowly and find out. All breeds can live very happily and safely with cats, but certain individuals might not be safe. It is not the breed as such but a natural tendency coupled with past experience (or lack of it). Consider also your dog's character – how does it react in stressful or unfamiliar situations? Does it get very excited and out of control; does it rush into things if it feels fearful? Your dog will have to be tolerant of this new little creature investigating it, its basket, its food, and, of course, its beloved owners. If you are at all unsure of your dog's reaction to this, take the trouble to make careful introductions so that it understands how it is allowed to act and what it is not allowed to do. Your dog may terrify the kitten or may itself be terrified of a confident kitten that has already met dogs and is not fazed by meeting another.

Most dogs chase cats because they are excited by the thrill of the hunt; they get caught up in the excitement and the chase rather than wanting to cause bodily harm just because it is a cat. Therefore chases are to be avoided at all costs.

Some dogs, especially those not used to cats or of an excitable or aggressive disposition, need extra-special care for introductions. They should be kept as calm as possible on the leash and made to sit quietly. The new cat should be given a safe position in the room and allowed to get used to the dog and approach it if it wants. This may take quite some time and requires patience and rewards for the dog if it behaves well. For quieter dogs and those used to cats, introductions can be made by using a strong cat carrier. Keep the dog on a leash initially, place the carrier on a high surface, and allow controlled interactions that are short and frequent. Most dogs will soon calm down when they realize the newcomer is not actually very interesting. Progress to meetings with the dog on the leash initially, for safety. If your dog is rather excitable, take it for a vigorous walk first to get rid of some of its energy!

Terriers or those breeds that like to chase, such as greyhounds, may need to be kept well under control until they have learned that the cat is not fair game! Young pups are likely to get very excited and may try to "play" with the new cat, which is unlikely to want to join in! You may need to work hard to keep things calm, and be aware that a sudden dash from the cat will induce a chase. Praise the dog for calm interactions, make it sit quietly, and use food treats to reward it for good behavior. Again, associate the presence of the cat with a reward for calm behavior. When you progress to meetings without the leash make sure there are places where the cat can escape to – high ledges or furniture it can use to feel safe. Never leave the dog and cat together unattended until you are sure they are safe together. The cat's food will be hugely tempting for any dog, so put it up and out of the way of thieving canine jaws! Likewise, a litter box can be pretty tempting and should be kept out of reach of the dog if it is likely to tamper with the contents.

INTRODUCING CATS TO CATS

Now this can be the hard one! Remember that cats do not need to be social creatures – unlike the pack-oriented dog, they function happily on their own without a social structure around them. They are unlikely to feel the need for a companion even though you might wish to have another cat around. You cannot force cats to like each other. Some will live with a newcomer easily, others will never get along or just manage to live alongside each other in an uneasy truce – you can only try. However, if there is no competition for food or safe sleeping places (as in most good homes), then cats will accept each other eventually. Some will even seem to form close bonds with one another.

While it may be a matter of feline choice as to whether cats get along, how you introduce a new cat or kitten into your home and to a resident cat or cats can make the difference between success or failure. Once a relationship becomes violent or very fearful and the cat feels threatened, it can be very difficult to change the behavior patterns. Thus, slow, careful introductions that prevent excessive reactions are vital. So what are the key factors involved in bringing cats together successfully?

Remember that scent is the most important of the cat's senses in terms of communication and well-being. You can try to integrate the new cat into your home and make it less alien by getting it to smell of "home" before you introduce it to the resident cat. To do this, stroke each cat without washing your hands to mix their scents. You can also gather scents from around the new cat's head area by gently stroking it with a soft cloth and dabbing the cloth around your home and furniture to mix and spread scents. Likewise, letting the cat get used to the new smells of the house and another cat before the initial meeting can make it more tolerable. For this reason it can be very useful to delay letting cats meet for a few days or even a week. During this time keep them in separate rooms, allowing each to investigate the other's room and bed without actually meeting.

It is up to you to make both the new cat and the resident feel as secure as possible and to prevent the newcomer from being chased or threatened (or occasionally the other way around). Problems can arise if initial meetings are allowed to deteriorate into a fight or chase. The best way to avoid this is to use a kitten pen for initial introductions. Kitten pens are metal mesh pens about 3.5 × 2.5 × 3.5 feet

$(1 \times 0.75 \times 1 \text{ m})$ with a door that can be left open or shut securely. The cat inside can see what is going on around it but feels safe inside its "den." You can put a blanket over the top initially to make the cat feel more secure if you think it feels vulnerable. The pen allows the cats to see each other, sniff through the bars, and hiss and moan at each other without any attack or intimidation. The bars allow them to be close together but provide protection at the same time.

If you have taken on a new kitten, a large pen can be very useful as a base for the kitten to be kept in initially. Introductions can be made using the pen, and you can shut the kitten in with its bed and litter box, if you are going out and don't want to leave it where it can get up to mischief or into danger. The kitten can be shut in the pen at night (ensure water is available) with the other animals in the same room, and they can get used to each other in safety.

If you can't find a pen or crate, you can use a cat carrier or basket for initial introductions. Of course, you won't be able to use it as a den to shut the cat or kitten in for long periods because it is too small, but it can be better than nothing.

Place the new cat or kitten in the pen/carrier and let the resident cat come into the room. If you are using a cat carrier, place it above ground level so the cats are not forced into direct eye contact with each other, which can cause aggression. Once the resident cat is in the room, give it attention and calm reassurance. If the cat decides to run away without investigating the new cat, do not force meetings. Accept that things may take a little time – this is probably the type of cat that will not initiate aggressive meetings but will stay out of the way and gradually accept the new cat in the household over time. If the cats show signs of aggression, distract them with a noise and then praise them for quiet encounters. You can use tidbits to encourage the cats to stay near each other, accept the other's presence, and make it a positive experience – you want the cats to associate each other with pleasant happenings, not shouting or chasing.

If you are using a large pen, you can allow the resident cat free access at times when the kitten/cat is in the pen so that they gradually get used to each other. If you are using a carrier, you will need to be a little more proactive and orchestrate frequent meetings. With both methods you can start to feed the cats at the same time, the resident outside and the new cat inside the pen or carrier on the floor. Throughout this process there may be some hissing and spitting, which should gradually change into curiosity and acceptance – this may take several days or weeks, depending on the individual cats.

When you feel the time is right to let them meet without the pen, you can again use food as a distraction. Withhold food so that they are somewhat hungry and then feed them in the same room. Choose a room where either cat can escape behind furniture, jump up high, or hide if it wants to. Put down the resident cat's food and then let the new cat out of its basket to eat. You will have to judge how close they can be – don't attempt to get them side by side initially! Be calm and reassuring and reward the behavior you want with praise and tidbits of a favorite food. Gauge how the cats are getting along – they may find their own spots and curl up to sleep, or you may need to keep the new one separate again for a little longer, using meals as a time for them to get together a bit more. Once you are sure they are not going to fight or chase, then you can start to utilize the whole house – the cats will probably find places to sleep and routines that allow them to live peacefully in the same house. They will partake of all the benefits of food, warmth, and attention while gradually becoming used to and accepting one another.

It may take only a day or two or as long as several weeks for cats to tolerate each other. It may take months before the cats are relaxed with each other, but you are on your way to success if they reach the stage of a calm truce. It is amazing how a cold, wet day outside will force even the worst adversaries together in front of the fire.

GROOMING

If you have taken on a long-haired or semi-long-haired cat, you will need to start handling your cat for grooming right from the beginning. Its coat may not yet be very long and may not even need too much combing, but it is much easier to let your kitten know that this is part of its life right at the beginning than to start when it is older and more difficult to influence. Little and often is the key; you can prevent tangles from forming if you groom for a short period and stop before the cat gets bored or fractious. Of course, if you have started early and in a kind, patient, and encouraging manner, your cat may love being groomed and you can keep it up for as long as you like. You want to avoid the scenario of feeling stressed and guilty because the cat with a beautiful flowing coat that you envisaged showing to your friends is actually a terrible sight, with knots and tangles and looking like it has been pulled through a hedge backwards. You don't want them to touch the knots of hair under the cat's tummy that it won't let you get to, and you would hate them to think you were a neglectful owner. However, despite all your best intentions, your cat makes it very difficult for you to get rid of the tangles.

Whatever coat type your kitten has, it is still useful to groom it – it makes it familiar with such handling, keeps the coat shiny, and allows you to keep a close eye on the cat's coat and skin. You will be able to see that it has lumps, bumps, parasites (such as ticks or fleas), or a dry or scabby coat. Along with the grooming, accustom your kitten to having its eyes and ears checked and its claws trimmed.

When you first start, it is essential that you do not cause any pain, pull the coat, or alarm the cat. Use a toothbrush around the face and work very gently. If you do find a knot, work slowly from above it, don't just drag the brush or comb through and pull on it. My children scream when I do this to their hair in the hurried moments before leaving for school, but I can explain to them it is because we are in a hurry and they should have done it themselves in the first place – I am usually forgiven. A bad experience for a kitten may mean that it comes to expect this every time the brush comes out. It is much better to associate the grooming equipment with a treat, gentle talk, and physical attention it likes, such as tickling under the chin or stroking on the head (my children would probably prefer this approach too!). If the kitten doesn't seem relaxed about you doing its tummy, approach the area in small chunks: do a little bit there, then do the head, and then a little bit more. Stop before it turns into a fight so that you end on a high and not on a low!

If you have a long-haired kitten, you will need to check the coat under the base of the tail and at the backs of the hindlegs to ensure it has not become soiled (especially when you first get it or are changing its diet, when it may suffer from a bit of diarrhea). Gently remove any soiling with a damp cotton ball so the kitten is clean and comfortable. Check between the kitten's toes and under its paws in case any litter from the litter box has become stuck there.

If you have one of the flatter-faced cats, such as Persians or Exotics, you may need to wipe its eyes on a regular basis, as the fluid that keeps the eyes moist cannot drain away properly through the tear ducts and spills out over the face. This can cause tear staining on the face at the inner corners of the eyes. Gently wipe this area with a cotton ball dampened with clean water or a little baby oil. Use a separate piece of cotton ball for each eye and dry with another cotton ball or a soft tissue. If you are going to do this every day, make sure it is a pleasant experience for the kitten – do not touch the eyeball, as this will be painful for the animal.

If you think your kitten's ears are grubby, do not use cotton swabs. Most veterinarians would advise you not to tamper with the ears at all, as the tissues lining the ear canals are very delicate and easily damaged. There may well be a reason that the ears are dirty – the kitten may have ear mites that are causing irritation and need to be tackled with medication from the veterinarian. Large deposits of wax in the ears or a reddening of the inner part of the ear may indicate a problem. If you want to wipe the outer part of the ear, use a cotton ball moistened with baby oil and never poke it down into the inner part of the ear itself.

If you intend to clip your cat's claws when it is older, perhaps because it is going to be an indoor cat and will not be going on hard surfaces or climbing trees that will blunt its claws, you will need to get the kitten used to the process. Invest in a pair of good-quality guillotine clippers – these usually have a small gap that goes around the claw and then closes to snip off the tip. Positioning is vital, though – you don't want to nick the little blood vessel that you will be able to see inside the claw. Make sure you cut beyond the spot where it disappears. Be confident and work efficiently so that it does not all end in a struggle. Kittens can be quite fidgety and you may initially need a couple of attempts before you actually do the cutting – stop if the kitten is getting agitated. As it gets used to its paw being held firmly and you get used to seeing what you are aiming at, you will get quicker and more confident.

Teach your kitten to let you look at its teeth and gums – again, this will stand you in good stead later on when it is grown and may be suffering from tartar or a gum problem. If you are very diligent, you may even consider cleaning your kitten's teeth. In an ideal world, we would all do this – your cat's teeth and oral health benefit from the same procedures that help humans maintain a healthy mouth. It is virtually impossible to start doing this with an adult cat; starting as young as possible is the only way. There are special feline toothbrushes and toothpastes that you can buy from your veterinarian – you might ask for a lesson in how best to do it at the same time.

Your kitten will have lost most of its baby (milk) teeth by about five months old, so don't panic if you notice a loose tooth or find one lying on the carpet. Check that there is no injury, just to be sure, but don't worry – another tooth will be growing through to take its place.

Of course, if you are at all worried about the health of your kitten, your veterinarian is the first port of call. You will need to take your kitten in either for vaccinations, neutering, or flea or worm treatments, so ask for a checkup at the same time. Chapter 10 goes into health matters in much more detail.

8

Training Your Kitten

We don't really think of ourselves as training our cats aside from litter training – which, in most cases, the mother cat has already done for us, so we can claim little credit there! Our relationship with dogs is based much more on the animal learning to do what it is asked or told to do. With cats it is usually the other way around. Wily beasts that they are, they very slowly and gently train their owners to do their bidding. Are there some lessons we can learn from how they work that might allow us to have a little control over them – or at least let us think we have trained them to do something?

Let's first think about why animals (and people for that matter) behave in certain ways. Like most living things, cats will do things because it benefits them to do so. Of course, it benefits them to get themselves out of situations that cause fear or pain, and they are then unlikely to put themselves in those situations again – not voluntarily, anyway. Therefore, if you want repetition of a behavior, you need the cat's cooperation and a desire to do it again. The cat needs to feel it is getting a reward for behaving in a certain way.

Punishment is not a good teaching tool. It will lead to resentment, fear, and stress for both the cat and the owner. Fear is a great inhibitor to learning. Some people may say that the cat knows it has done wrong when, for example, it scratches the wallpaper or sprays indoors. This is not so – it may associate the action with you behaving in a very irrational fashion, jumping about and screaming or attacking it, but none of this will make it feel guilty – merely confused and scared. The link between the owner's anger and the behavior is rarely made by the animal. All it succeeds in doing is breaking down the relationship. If the behaviors were first carried out as a natural response to the way the cat was feeling – perhaps frightened or threatened by another cat – punishment will do nothing to put this right, but rather will give the cat more to worry about. There are ways of interrupting behaviors you do not want without associating negative things with you as a loving owner who should be providing an environment to encourage confidence, not conflict and fear.

And remember, a cat is not a dog. A dog is a pack-oriented animal. It has a behavior repertoire that allows it to compromise, to give in, and still be accepted within the pack. Being part of the pack is all important, and the dog will remain within the pack even if it receives punishment. So we can train dogs using all the wrong methods of fear and threat, and they will probably give in and do as they are asked. They may not carry out the tasks with much enthusiasm and will go through life feeling fearful, but they feel a strong need to stay and compromise if possible. Cats are a different matter altogether. While they can be sociable if they want to, when it comes down to it, a cat walks on its own. There is no support group to hunt with or to defend it – it is responsible for its own survival and safety. It does not have a great behavioral repertoire for compromise and will not be motivated to stay where it feels threatened and uncomfortable. You need to think in a much more clever way when you deal with cats. If you use the same thinking for dogs and work with reward instead of punishment, you will find they respond exceptionally well. They will work hard to gain reward for the task as well as the reward of fitting into a stable and predictable place within the pack – making a contented and happy dog.

So: think reward. Rewards for cats come in many shapes and forms, and what is great for one kitten may not move another. Going back to dogs for a moment, getting the reward right is easier – a great many dogs are very, very motivated by food. They crave attention and a place in the pack, and many are bred – and so have a drive – to undertake certain tasks. Allowing them to undertake these tasks – such as retrieving or scent-following – will be a reward in itself. We have all seen working dogs having a great time undertaking tasks that suit them. Ask a greyhound to retrieve or a Labrador to run around a track and you might not be so successful!

What can we offer cats? Some of them enjoy food or certain treats; some crave attention; others want only play. Punishment will get you nowhere, so you cannot force them, as we might be able to do with dogs, or people for that matter. Think about how we train different animals: how would you punish a killer whale if it doesn't leap high enough? Once again, more thinking and less forcing is required. So while as a race we revert to punishment out of frustration only too often, we have to rise above this, learn something about motivation, and act in a way that is much more rewarding all around. With cats you need to be much more cerebral and use much less force! This characteristic will make training your kitten both challenging and very rewarding. If you can train your cat, you can use the techniques on the children or the dog and find it easy – you will have thought through what the pupil might want, learned how to motivate him, and then honed your timing skills so that your pupil knows the reward is for the action you intended. A very good start!

As this stage, you may be asking, "Why would I want to train my cat?" Yes, you could train it to do tricks, but most of us feel that cats are far too dignified to do that. When dealing with such an elegant and independent animal (the very reasons why most of us have cats), training should be sensitive and fun, and there are practical reasons for doing a little bit of it. What you are aiming to do is to train your kitten to respond to you. It is very useful to be able to call your kitten to come to you and to be able to communicate to it which behaviors are appropriate in the house and which are not. Training will also strengthen the bond between you and your cat – it will make you look at each other in a slightly different way. Studying what works between you and what doesn't can prove very useful in keeping your cat stimulated and active. It can also be a great confidence booster for you both. You will begin to think about new ways of reinforcing behaviors and successes. Good relationships between any two individuals, be they people or a person and an animal, are based on mutual respect and good communication. And this requires intelligent thought. Using kind, gentle, and effective training methods should result in a meeting of minds; if you succeed, you have really started to understand how cats think. Of course, in order to do this, you might need to do a little homework about cats, how they communicate, how they see the world, and what their natural reactions are – there is some information on this in Chapter 12, but you may need to gather more books on cat behavior to really grasp it.

What motivates a kitten to learn – especially to learn something you want it to do that is new to its repertoire? Cats, not being slave-like creatures, will rarely do something for nothing. You will have to find something special, something you know it loves – a prawn, a bit of cheese or chicken, or a liver-flavored treat. It's no good offering a bit of dry cat food from the bowl, which it can eat any time it likes. It would be like offering you a slice of bread as a reward for learning how to do your tax return – lobster and champagne might be nearer the mark. Various treats are available at the pet shop or supermarket; find one your kitten loves but don't give in to the temptation to use it all the time. Save treats for maximum motivating! Some cats are not at all motivated by food of any kind but may respond to playing with a particular toy or being talked to and stroked in a certain way. A good motivator is really essential in the initial stages of training.

Once you have found your motivating tool, you have to learn about timing. As in comedy, timing is all-important when it comes to rewarding your pet. You have to provide the reward and the kitten has to be aware of it as soon as it performs the desired behavior. The kitten needs to make the connection between what it has done and the thing it wants, so that it associates the behavior with something rather nice. A delay of even a second may destroy the connection and the kitten will not get the message – that will be your fault, not the kitten being slow to learn.

Next you have to think carefully about what you want your kitten to do. Again, think about the task from the kitten's point of view. If you want to teach it to use the cat flap, realize that it will not know that if you push hard enough on this seemingly solid object, you will make it open up. It will not understand that it can climb through and not have to worry as it closes on its tail! Always break the task down into as many small stages as possible and work toward achieving each step in a quiet and methodical way. Visiting Sea World in Florida I saw a spectacular trick in which one of the killer whales swam beneath a trainer and came up underneath his feet extremely fast, pushing him out of the water with his nose. The trainer shot up – the force with which he was propelled was extremely impressive. I wondered how many steps it had taken to get that right. Getting it wrong could also be extremely dangerous. And while a cat is not a killer whale, it is almost impossible to rush a cat – any impatience on your part will just turn it off from trying altogether. You don't get away with being a bad trainer with a cat, either.

Choose a time when there are no distractions so you can both concentrate – children, dogs, and other cats may try to join in if they think the kitten is the center of attention, so prepare the time and place and have your reward at the ready. Don't try to grab five minutes between cooking the dinner, answering the phone, and getting the kids to bed. Take care of all that, take a deep breath, and then consider it. See what mood the kitten is in. All of us have times of the day (or whole days) when we don't want to concentrate or try anything new. At other times we are very excited about learning. The same can be said for you, the trainer – don't do it if you are feeling grumpy or short-tempered: you could do more harm than good.

Likewise, if the kitten seems tired, overexcited, or just bored, just try a couple of times and give up on a high if you can. Have you ever found that when you try something for the first time it is very difficult, but on coming back and trying again the next day it doesn't seem half so bad? This is known as latent learning – the gap between first attempting the new behavior and then returning to it with a greater understanding the next time. It can be very helpful in training and reassuring to you if you think that you haven't achieved anything – you may get more done by trying short, enjoyable sessions with breaks in between.

TRAINING TO COME WHEN CALLED

We don't want our cats to be obedient like dogs, and most of the time we don't need them to be. Dogs can cause trouble and can be dangerous, so there is a need to ensure they are under control. However, it can be very useful if your cat comes running when you want it, or at least responds by meowing or trying in some way to get to you. If it does become lost or shut in a room, such a response can save a great deal of heartache and help you find it much more easily. You will also be able to locate it for the everyday things, such as feeding or bringing it inside and locking the cat flap at night. This training is also vital for when you let your kitten out for the first time into the big, wide world. And, let's face it, it is really lovely if you call your cat and it comes running across the yard to greet you.

Food is probably the best thing to use to motivate your kitten, and training it to associate its name with getting a treat is a good start. Therefore, start with the food ready and the kitten nearby, when it is not too distracted by something else. Call its name and immediately offer it the tidbit. Keep your voice light and encouraging and offer food every time you call its name. According to experts, a two-syllable word seems to have more of an activating effect on animals, while single, flatter tones have a calming or slowing effect. Perhaps this is because, with two syllables, you can say the name in a more singsong sort of way and end on a high note, which has the promise of something good. Perhaps this is why many people choose cat names with a "y" or "ie" at the end and automatically call Smokie or Bonny or Sandy in that way. Remember to reward immediately.

You want your kitten to get it right, so don't expect it to make great leaps of achievement. Call it from slightly longer distances, but still in sight, until it has really got the hang of it. Then you can try it from just outside the room or around the corner. Instead of rewarding with food every time, try giving praise or playing with a favorite toy. See if that is an acceptable reward for your particular kitten.

If you want to sharpen your kitten's response so that it comes to you faster, try rewarding only the best responses.

Never do what you may have seen so many dog owners do. Having lost the dog or having seen it go off in search of a fight or a friend, they call frantically. When it does come back they punish it, venting their frustration and embarrassment on the dog. What does the dog learn from this? Don't come back or expect something unpleasant if you do. That's why many of them come back in that submissive posture, asking to be let off. Cats don't really have a submissive posture, so they just don't bother at all! Never punish the kitten after calling it. And remember that punishment may not just mean shouting or hitting – it may mean putting the kitten in the car or into a carrier associated with the veterinarian and being caught and sprayed for fleas. Make sure you leave a little time between rewarding it for coming and doing what you need to do with the kitten. One bad experience can undo weeks of positive training – again, you need to think like a cat and realize how you may be perceived.

WEARING A COLLAR OR HARNESS AND WALKING ON A LEASH

If you want your kitten to wear a collar or a harness (if you want it to walk on a leash), it's best to start early. Choose a soft collar or harness with no pieces that the kitten can get itself tangled up in or in which it might tangle up its claws. Fit the collar properly – see page 164 for a discussion on types of collars and fitting them correctly. Leave it on for only a little while and don't leave the kitten unattended with it on. Distract it with play or food so that it almost doesn't notice it has the collar on. If it gets distressed it may almost turn itself inside out trying to get it off, so don't let it get frantic.

A few seconds may be enough at the beginning. Remember about latent learning and try again later – if the first time wasn't too bad it will react less next time… and so on. Gradually extend the period that the collar or harness is worn in the house, taking your cues from the kitten. You want the end result to be complete relaxation while wearing it. This may take some time to achieve.

Use a harness if you want to train the kitten to walk on a leash – the harness won't pull on its neck and, if the cat does panic, it won't strangle itself. Get it used to the harness in the same way as the collar. Once it has become used to the harness you can think about attaching the leash. Exercising a dog is not the same as walking a cat on a harness. With a dog you control where it goes; usually with a cat on a harness you follow the cat. I have seen people walking cats on leashes in some very public places such as parks, and the cats do seem to be going the same way as the person and not the other way around. So it is possible – though I suspect it takes quite an exceptional cat and some patient training. For most of us, just being able to give an indoor cat a stretch outside in the fresh air in safety is probably enough.

Remember, when a cat feels threatened, its automatic response is not to turn and fight but to get itself away from the situation as quickly as possible and without harm. If it is suddenly stopped from running, it may well panic and become very frightened. It needs to learn to accept the feeling of restraint and not to panic about it.

Getting your kitten used to being restricted must be done very carefully. Attach a lightweight piece of string or cord to the harness so that the kitten can get used to having something there. Hold the end gently and allow your kitten to walk a little – the best way is to tempt it with some food in your other hand. If the kitten moves away, follow it calmly. Never let the cord pull on the kitten – if it makes a sudden dash and you are not quick enough to follow, drop the cord. Don't let the kitten play with the other end. The kitten may wind it up, pull on the harness, and frighten itself as it becomes restricted.

Once the kitten is happy with the cord and you following, try attaching a lightweight leash – this will be heavier and will have a different feel on the harness. Again, short sessions aided by praise and reward for the kitten's relaxed demeanor are what you are looking for. Once you feel you have accomplished this you can think about going outside. Of course, you are not doing this with a very young kitten, so by the time you are ready for harness work outside your kitten will have been fully vaccinated.

Choose a quiet time and venture only into the yard. Ensure that the dog walker with the noisy terrier that lunges at everything as it passes has had its walk, and that next door's pushy tomcat is not hiding under the bush near the door. You want to avoid anything that will give the kitten a shock and make it want to run off. Going outside will be exciting enough. Again, short excursions every now and then will do the trick.

TRAINING TO USE THE CAT FLAP

Once your kitten has had all its vaccinations, you may decide you want it to go outside and that you would like it to be able to use a cat flap. If you already have a cat flap, your kitten will be familiar with the sight of it. Indeed, if you have an older cat that uses the flap, be careful – kittens learn by watching and many a kitten has presumed that it can do whatever the big cat can do. You think the kitten is safely shut inside because you have not yet taught it to use the flap and suddenly there it is, out in the yard! However, if it has no feline tutor, you will have to step in.

A cat flap can be quite a scary thing – it looks solid yet swings about and often makes quite a clunk or even a snap as it shuts. The door touches the body as the cat goes through and often almost shuts on the tail. On going through, the kitten is very exposed for a few moments because it cannot see what is on the other side and it cannot run away.

There are a host of cat flaps to choose from, but it is best to choose one that can lock in either or both ways. If you have a high density of cats in the area and don't want all of them visiting you (and terrorizing your kitten), consider getting one that is triggered to open by a magnet that is carried on the cat's collar. A similar cat flap is made to open by an electronic key on the collar. In this way you can be selective about which felines you welcome in.

By now you will have realized that grabbing your kitten and forcing it through the flap as it panics is not the best approach. It may never want to go near it again. Breaking the exercise into smaller chunks will be slower but much more effective. Your kitten needs to understand that the flap is a method of gaining entrance to or exit from its home – it can open the way to adventure or, if coming in, to security. The first thing to do is to prop the door open with a pencil or stick it open with some tape – use any method you like to fix the door horizontally open and leave the largest hole possible for the kitten to look through. Of course, if you are letting the kitten see the real outdoors for the first time, it is likely to be very wary. It might be easier to let it enter the area it is familiar with, letting it tackle the cat flap from the outside first. Hold the kitten just outside the door looking in. Get another member of the family or a friend to encourage it from the inside with a treat or a toy and by calling its name. Remember to reward the kitten as soon as it comes through the hole.

Once the kitten has mastered coming in through the hole, try going the other way. Call it from the outside. Again, reward it as it comes through.

The next step is to prop the door so that it is only half open. The kitten will still be able to see out and know that it can go through, but it will have to push the door a little and feel it on its back as it goes through. Encourage the kitten to push and come through and then reward it. Try the exercise from both sides before putting the door down a bit further and repeating the process. In no time at all the kitten will be confidently barreling through the flap and enjoying its freedom.

What about when you want to lock the door at night to keep the kitten safely indoors – won't that confuse it? The way to overcome this is to place a signal or sign there that only appears when the door is locked. You could just use a piece of board or material in front of the flap so that the kitten learns that, when this is present, it is futile to try getting through. Be consistent with your signage – you can gradually use it less and less once the kitten understands that the flap is shut only at certain times and open at others.

RETRIEVING

The Feline Advisory Bureau Cat Personality Survey referred to earlier in this book found that **44** percent of owners said that their cats retrieved. Just under half of these said that their cats retrieved frequently, the rest occasionally. Breeds such as Siamese, Burmese, Tonkinese, Somali, Ragdoll, and Rex were well represented in these frequent retrievers, and the cats tended to be younger if they were moggies (less than five years old). The retrieved objects included beads, feathers, paper balls, string, cotton spools, leaves, socks, and brushes. Carrying prey is a natural behavior for cats, as is bringing it back to a base; for example, to feed kittens, or just to eat it in safety. Of course, this is all done for the cat's benefit or, in some cases, to benefit its kittens. Most of the people in the survey didn't set out to train their cats – it simply happened as they played. We know that some breeds such as Siamese and Burmese are more interactive than other breeds as well as moggies, and we know that younger cats are often likely to interact for attention or the enjoyment of chasing and playing. Thus, in most of these cases I suspect it has been the cat that has trained its owners – they have thrown a toy, and the cat has returned it and found that if it gives them the toy, they will throw it again, encouraging and reacting to the cat every time it brings the toy – it is a great attention grabber.

Playing retrieve is a great way to exercise and build bonds with your kitten. It can be especially important when cats are going to be kept indoors all the time and will not get the stimulation, exercise, and adventures associated with going outdoors.

If you want to encourage your cat to retrieve, select a toy in which it has shown interest, and use the toy in play. Choose one that the cat can actually carry easily, something that is not too heavy and which fits easily in the cat's mouth. If the cat has no particular interest in a toy, choose one for it and perhaps smear the toy with some of the cat's favorite food to catch its interest.

As soon as your kitten runs after the toy and picks it up, call it to you. Offer a treat or an identical toy as a swap for the one it has picked up. Don't force the kitten to let go or have a game of tug-of-war. You will only encourage it to run off with the toy the next time so that you do not even get a chance to grab it. Repeat the exercise and the kitten will soon get the idea – many really enjoy the interaction and the chance to run off some of that kitten energy.

A method of training called clicker training has become well known in dog training and also works for cats. The idea is to indicate to the animal the exact action that has earned the reward. This is done with a clicker – a small plastic box containing a flexible steel plate that makes a double-click sound when pressed. It is a very distinctive sound and can be made very quickly, marking the behavior you are pinpointing very accurately. It is much better than a voice and, once the cat has made the association between the click and the reward, the animal understands that the click marks the correct behavior and the reward will follow. In the end the click will suffice as the reward itself.

TRAINING YOUR KITTEN WHAT NOT TO DO

OK, we can motivate cats to do what we want – what about when they do things we don't want? In general, behaviors that go unrewarded will become less and less frequent over time – there is little point in the cat investing energy in an action if it brings no benefit. However, once again we need to think about the nature of the reward. If a cat scratches the wallpaper, it may be as a response to a feeling of threat from another cat and a need to mark its territory to improve its own confidence – the reward is the feeling it gets from carrying out a behavior it is highly motivated to do. Without removing the cause of the problem (for example, the threat from another cat coming into the house), it is difficult to change the behavior. You may be able to move it onto a more appropriate surface, such as a scratch post, but you need to understand where to put it and why. You need to think like a cat.

In general it is easier to train your kitten to do things than not to do them, especially if something has already become a learned habit. Prevention, as usual, is better than cure. Punishment, whether physical or only vocal, will be associated with the last event that occurred (which, of course, is not usually the one that has caused the anger), and the kitten will be very confused about your aggressive behavior.

Many problems are brought on by owners themselves being inconsistent and sometimes by inadvertently teaching the kitten something wrong in the first place. It is important to be consistent from the start and not to allow your kitten to do things you would not accept from an adult cat. Letting your kitten bite and scratch you may be quite funny when it is tiny – you will not appreciate it as it grows into a cat. Many people encourage this by tickling the kitten's tummy and being amused as it grabs their hands – men are particularly good at these games that push kittens a little too far! Of course, it will be the children who get grabbed rather too hard by the growing kitten in play. It has not learned that it does not get attention if it gets rough – on the contrary, it has been encouraged to act in this way and rewarded with heaps of attention.

If you don't want your cat on the work surfaces in the kitchen, don't let the kitten go there and don't leave food out that acts as a reward should the kitten find it there, making it worth exploration in the future. Lift the kitten down each time and praise it for being on the ground.

If you want to be awakened at 5 A.M. every morning with demands for food and play, by all means get up and give the kitten attention. It then cannot be blamed for depriving you of a good night's sleep. Giving in only once a week is enough to reward the kitten and give it the signal that it is worth the effort of waking you.

Finally, don't train your kitten to avoid the litter box by using it as a spot to give medicine.

HOW DO CATS TRAIN US?

Your kitten is a very bright little character. It is on a steep learning curve and is making new discoveries every day. It learns by watching, by trial and error, and by the reactions you give it to things that it does. It learns which of its actions result in something it likes and which don't. In particular, it learns how to make you do what it wants (just like any child worth its salt!). It is up to you to decide when you are to be manipulated, when you want to be manipulated because it is actually what you want as well, and when you definitely do not want to give in!

Cats are amazing teachers – most of us know we are the slaves of a cat rather than the owners. Just think of the ways your cat trains you. If it wants attention it puts on its best strutting walk with its tail up high, rubs around your legs, looks at you, and meows. Anyone with even a small affection for cats will immediately be stroking and smiling and asking the cat what it wants! How many people do actually get up at 5 A.M. because the cat wants something? Lots! And kittens, cute though they are, are not the ultimate masters of this. It is older cats that have got things really slick! I know of one that has to be tucked into bed with a hot-water bottle wrapped in a towel. When the bottle gets cold it calls down for its owner, who obediently adds more hot water and tucks the cat into bed again!

Cats can do this because their affection rewards us – they do not have to offer food, just a meow or a purr of praise and we are putty in their hands. They seldom revert to aggression but rather give us a slow drip, drip, drip of reward for our attention – that's the way to do it!

9

Your Kitten's Lifestyle

Having got your kitten (or kittens) home you may already have decided what type of lifestyle it is going to have. If you live in a typical urban or suburban area or if your home is in an apartment, townhouse, or condominium, you will probably not want your feline friends to venture outdoors because of traffic and other dangers. In the United States most pet cats are kept within the confines of the home because of the high risk of death from poisons, contagious diseases, accidents, infected cat bite wounds, attacks by dogs, and simply wandering too far in unfamiliar surroundings. Two cats will keep each other company and provide some stimulation to each other. If you live in a rural setting, on a farm or ranch, and your cats' principal function is to keep down the pest level, this information doesn't apply to you. This chapter outlines some of the risks and benefits of outdoor and indoor cats and provides advice for the decision you must make.

The majority of cat owners in Great Britain give their feline companions freedom to come and go as they please. However, more and more are deciding to keep their cats completely indoors. In the United States residents are encouraged to keep their feline pets inside. This brings up a number of questions. Are indoor cats better off, or is it an unnatural hardship for cats to be kept indoors? Indoor cats usually live longer and physically healthier lives than cats allowed outdoors but are housebound cats more likely to suffer psychologically and develop behavioral problems than cats allowed outside? Do indoor cats suffer from the effects of drugs used to control behavioral problems caused by confinement? Indoor cats may also suffer from obesity without enough exercise.

It wasn't until the advent of cat litter in the 1950s that cat owners had much choice about letting their cats out. Before that time, cats had to spend at least part of their days and sometimes all night outside. I'm not sure why putting the cat out at night became the right thing for cat owners. Perhaps it stems from the days when cats were expected to keep down the vermin population and were let out to do their nocturnal jobs.

Cats had to go outside to go to the toilet, and had to wait until somebody let them back into the house because many owners did not have cat doors. Now some indoor cats are trained to use human toilets but so far no one has trained them to flush.

The home is often empty of people during the day so there is nobody to let cats in and out. That situation demands either a litter box or special training in order for the cats to stay indoors, but is the situation more complicated than that? Outdoor cats may go out through their cat door whenever they choose to do so and thus decide their own routines and limits, but they are also at risk to some dangers in the great outdoors. The main risks are outlined below:

- Automobile accidents account for many cat deaths every year. If you live in a town or near a busy road, then the risks are probably greater, although quiet roads can sometimes be as dangerous because cats may not look out for traffic.

- Dog attacks can be debilitating or fatal and cat bites often abscess and require veterinary intervention at a significant cost. In rural areas wild predators often kill and eat cats. Neighbors may injure unwanted feline visitors.

- Contact with sick feral cats can lead to potentially fatal infections; for example, feline immunodeficiency virus, feline leukemia virus, cat flu, or feline enteritis viruses.

- Pesticides, herbicides, fungicides, creosote, antifreeze, and other common chemicals can be toxic or even fatal if consumed by cats. Eating poisoned rodents can be harmful.

- Fleas, ticks, mites, worms, and other parasites can be picked up from eating their prey and from the environment.

- Some cats disappear for days or sometimes permanently. They can get shut in garages or climb into trucks and vans and be driven away from home. They may occasionally move in with someone else if they find a better option or if there is something at home causing stress, such as another cat.

- A timid cat may find the great outdoors very stressful and prefer to be inside. This is always a good type of cat to keep indoors because it is there by choice!

However, there are benefits to letting your cat go outdoors unsupervised:

- Outdoor cats are usually well exercised by hunting and patrolling their territory or playing. They are less likely to become overweight and bored from inactivity.

- Outdoor cats may receive social stimulation through positive and negative interaction with other cats in the area. However, those cats must think on their feet and act quickly to take part in the uncertainty of life outside.

- Rodent control in today's urban and suburban society is not the problem it was in the middle ages. However, if you have a serious rodent problem in your neighborhood, a good feline hunter or two will keep the rodent population at bay.

- Genetic traits such as territory marking, claw sharpening, and play-hunting are all inherent feline behaviors that must be adjusted for indoor cats. Owners of indoor cats must encourage their cats to exercise and should furnish toys and equipment to satisfy those needs.

- Outdoor cats are less likely to develop behavioral problems such as inappropriate urination in the house, spraying, clawing furniture, or stalking humans or other household pets.

MINIMIZING THE RISKS FOR THE OUTDOOR CAT

- If you let your cat outside, try to do so during the daylight hours because predators are more abundant at night. Dark, cloudy, or moonless nights are a real problem especially for dark colored cats that aren't easily seen. A reflective or fluorescent collar may help your cat to be seen, particularly in winter months when it gets dark earlier. A flashing reflection may help your feline friend to be seen by motorists but it also makes him more visible to predators.

- Good timing is important. If you live near a busy road, encourage your cat to come in during high-traffic times. However, such habits are more difficult to develop than you might think.

- Vaccinations are critical. Be sure that your cat is vaccinated against all infectious diseases possible. Unfortunately, there is no vaccine for FIV. Have routine worm tests performed because successful hunters often become re-infected regularly.

- Identification is problematical. If your cat wears a collar, make sure the collar has a safety catch that will snap open if it gets caught on tree limbs, thereby enabling your cat to escape without injury. Write your name and phone number clearly on the collar so that anyone who finds your sick or injured cat can let you know. A microchip the size of a grain of rice carrying a unique number can be injected under the skin. A cat taken to a shelter or veterinary hospital can be scanned and the microchip numbers matched to the address on file. Cats can also be tattooed but the numbers and letters may become blurred over time.

- Neutering is extremely important. Have your female cat spayed or your male cat castrated. The risks associated with intact animals are much greater than those associated with neutered ones. An unneutered tom or unspayed female will wander for miles looking for prospective mates. Neutered cats do not wander as far or fight as much as intact cats and therefore are not at such a great risk of being infected with various diseases. Neutered cats aren't the nuisances of yowling toms or queens, and don't cause the foul odors that your neighbors hate so much. The risks of pregnancy to the unneutered female are also obvious.

THE INDOOR CAT

- Keeping a cat permanently indoors away from all the potential hazards outside may sound like the ideal solution. However, the benefits of safety should be weighed against the needs of your pet.

- There might be more stress-linked psychological problems in indoor cats. Behavioral or anxiety-related problems such as urine marking might possibly have a higher incidence in the United States than in the

United Kingdom. That could be because British cats are allowed outside more often than cats in the United States.

- Fear of change may be a problem of indoor cats that become overreactive to changes within their small territory. Confined cats become unable to cope with changes in their environment whether the change involves new people, objects, or smells. It can be difficult to introduce a new cat (or even a new spouse) into your cat's restricted territory because there is no neutral ground to retire to for either party.

- Obesity related to lack of exercise can lead to health problems but in an otherwise healthy cat obesity usually can be handled nutritionally and by furnishing more interesting toys to play with.

- Overdependence is a problem of a single indoor cat that relies on its owner to provide stimulation, companionship, and exercise. That problem is sometimes solved by the addition of a compatible cat to the household. Some very active and sociable breeds such as the Siamese or Burmese can become extremely attached or bonded to their owners. They sleep during the day when their owner is not around. When their owner is present, the cats become very demanding. Some owners enjoy the intensity of this relationship but it is very difficult for the cat because when its owner is away the cat may become stressed. Those cats may over-groom themselves under such circumstances. At first the cat grooms itself normally, which is known to relieve tension. If the cat grooms for longer periods to try to achieve further relaxation, the grooming may become obsessive. Sometimes cats develop bald patches where they have literally licked off the fur.

• Damage to your furniture and carpets from being scratched excessively will occur if you fail to provide ample scratching posts or mats. However, regardless of whether or not they are confined, all kittens climb, jump, and generally whiz around the house in mad moments of frenzied activity. That is simply part of being a kitten and will usually pass in about a year or two with help from training.

• Keeping doors and windows shut so indoor cats can't escape can be very difficult with children around. Usually warning the kids about the dangers of the outdoors to their cherished kitten is sufficient.

• Boredom and curiosity can be a dangerous combination and it often occurs in half grown kittens. Washing machines, toilets, medicines, cleaners, household chemicals of all kinds, small holes, exposed wires, and loose shelving are hazards for curious kittens, whether they are indoor or outdoor cats.

- Accidental poisoning is possible from ornamental backyard or indoor plants. Cats often crave greenery and nibble at whatever grass, plants, or herbs are available. Outdoor cats have an abundance of harmless plants and a few deadly ones to choose from. Some indoor plants are also dangerous but those are easily identified and can be put out of reach or eliminated by the concerned owner.

- Escape of an indoor cat that gets outside may be dangerous if he becomes disoriented and afraid. A confused kitten wandering about a strange neighborhood is an easy target for predators. Some cats fall from their high-rise dwelling because of unprotected balconies or windows. Sometimes indoor cats become frustrated because they can't escape from poorly trained children or household pets. For this reason, a safe refuge must be supplied to all cats. Those problems exist whether the cat is inside a few hours a day or 24 hours every day.

- Frustration or boredom can sometimes show itself in what is called redirected aggression. If an indoor cat sees another cat in the backyard or is stimulated by an unidentified movement, he may become excited and frustrated, and then panic. If the owner happens to be available at the time, the cat may attack because he is aroused and because most activity is already focused on his owner.

BENEFITS OF KEEPING CATS INDOORS

- Indoor cats historically encounter fewer risks to their physical health. They usually live longer, more comfortable lives because they are protected from the diseases and accidents associated with the outside world.

- Parasites are not a significant problem for indoor cats because humans and other animals rarely bring in fleas or internal parasites. Once an indoor cat is free from infestation, he should not suffer from re-infestation.

- Happy neighbors don't complain about your indoor cat because he doesn't use children's sandboxes, vegetable patch, or flower garden as a litter box. He doesn't yowl or cause fights and is rarely visible.

- With no access to the outside world, your indoor cat won't hunt and bring its prey into the house, and you won't be faced with the unpleasantness of cleaning up animal corpses on the carpet.

HOW CAN YOU HELP THE INDOOR CAT?

The main problem faced by an indoor cat is lack of opportunity to do those things that come naturally, such as hunting. An outdoor cat hunts for a living rather than being fed gourmet foods by us humans. He will eat between seven and fifteen small meals a day and may have to go through the hunting sequence 150 times to catch this many entrees. That demands a lot of concentrated activity and a lot of prey. If he doesn't have this energy outlet and if he is a dedicated predator, he may become bored and frustrated and develop behaviors to compensate in some way for his lack of fulfillment. The owner must accept responsibility and produce new toys and games to keep the cat stimulated and exercised, both physically and mentally. Kittens and cats love newspaper tents, cardboard boxes, and paper bags, not to mention various cat play centers, fishing rod toys, and laser lights. Those toys encourage stalking and pouncing but you can't just supply these resources. You need to be proactive and initiate play and hunting activities. So while you may have chosen a cat because it is an easier option than a dog, an indoor cat does require a lot of your time.

The intensity of his hunting games may gradually lessen as he gets older. A cat's enthusiasm is greatest at between one and two years. At that age he is the equivalent of a 15- to 24-year-old human. Humans of that age range have lots of energy to burn and enjoy sports and physical activities. They are less fearful of danger and welcome the challenges. It is the same with young cats. They are naturally very fit and athletic and want to get out there and use their talents. We all know that our dogs need to be exercised or they can be very difficult to live with. They may become destructive, noisy, or aggressive because they have not expended their energy. Probably a good case exists for environmental enrichment programs for indoor cats, which includes placing their food in toys or balls that have to be moved about to get access to the food. Initiate a game wherein your cat's food is hidden so that he must hunt for it. Some breeders who keep their cats indoors for health reasons provide large exercise wheels for them, and the cats apparently love them because they give a chance to burn off some energy.

If you intend to keep your cat indoors, it is a good idea to start out with two kittens instead of one. Another cat of a similar age will bring company, a changing environment, and interaction. This is most important in a small, totally indoor situation. However, it may be difficult to introduce a new kitten into the home of an older and established indoor cat because there are few places to hide or get away from each other. You may cause more stress than you relieve. Having two kittens will help you to resolve your guilt feelings associated with leaving one lonesome kitten to amuse itself while you are at work. Having two kittens relieves you of some of the burden of having to stimulate and provide exercise because two kittens will happily wear each other out playing and then collapse in a heap to sleep. They will, however, need somewhere safe to play and you may need to spend more time making sure your house is kitten safe.

When the cat's whole world consists of a couple of rooms in an apartment that he knows inside out, he can become hypersensitive to change. Thus, you must continually introduce small changes so that the cat remains able to adapt. Make sure that you have regular visitors and life is not too quiet, especially when your kitten is small. A new baby, new pet, or even temporary workmen in the home will be perceived as significant changes in the household routine and can produce a potentially huge alteration to the cat's perception of its daily environment, resulting in stress. Remember that the environment and experiences of youth shape what your cat will continue to recognize as normal when he is an adult.

Indoor cats, especially young ones, might have quite an adverse impact on your furniture. Drapes offer a challenge to a young adventuresome kitten with sharp climbing skills. Try not to be too house-proud about the ensuing damage. Prevent rather than regret. Move all the knickknacks, temporarily tie up the drapes, trim toenails nice and short, and pretend that you have a toddler that can fly! Provide a safe place where cats can have a "free for all."

Your cat will act out its natural behavioral activities such as sharpening claws within your home. Outdoor cats can use a tree or fence post but an indoor cat must be provided with a good scratching post, a large piece of tree bark, or a floor or doorknob scratching mat. Even with those he is likely to use the furniture occasionally.

Monitor your cat's food intake and weigh him occasionally if you think he's putting on excess pounds. If he is getting fat and his weight gain isn't stopped by feeding less and he doesn't use interactive toys and takes no exercise through play, take him to your veterinarian for an examination. Several dangerous diseases are signaled by weight gain.

A cat that goes outdoors will nibble on grass and herbs as part of its diet. It is believed that eating vegetation helps cats to regurgitate hairballs. You can overcome the vegetable deficit in his diet by providing him with an indoor window box. Grass, catnip, thyme, sage, parsley, or wheat and oats can be sown indoors in a potting mixture. Sow more seeds in a new window box every couple of weeks to provide a fresh supply for your cat.

Invest in some good nail clippers, as your cat's hind claws may not wear down as quickly as they would if he went outside and walked on hard surfaces. Long claws can become snagged in carpets and upholstery.

Cat-proof your home carefully. An inquisitive kitten can get though a very small hole. If you live several stories up, put screens over the windows and train everyone in the family to keep doors shut.

A HAPPY MEDIUM?

Many owners are now investing in outdoor runs for their cats. This may be an enclosed walkway in the backyard so the cats can get some fresh air and have somewhere to lie in the sun and watch everything that goes on in the yard. It may be a permanent fixture or a moveable structure that can be changed to different areas of the yard. A strong outdoor enclosure with a safe, secure refuge-house could provide your cat with the sights and smells of the outside world and give its life some variety without exposing it to outdoor risks. Alternatively you might consider using high fencing and squirrel guards on trees to keep your cat within the confines of your backyard. You may decide to train your cat or kitten to walk on a harness and leash so you can both take safe walks about the neighborhood.

CAT CHARACTERS

Some cats will adapt more readily to an indoor lifestyle than others. A cat that has spent half its life living outdoors may not readily accept an indoor life. In the United States veterinarians say that some cats won't adjust to this change and suggest a program of behavior modification to enable the animal to get over the problems that arise. This often includes temporary treatment with anxiety-reducing drugs. However, when the cause of the stress is not being able to go outside, a temporary course of these drugs is unlikely to work.

On the other hand, many mild-mannered cats are quite happy to stay indoors and avoid the circumstances that they find very stressful. A controlled and predictable indoor environment may be ideal, and often cats with other options choose not to venture outdoors a great deal anyway.

Once again it depends on the character of your cat. You may have a rough and ready character that pines for large, open spaces and physical activity, or your cat may be a curious little feline friend who is so inquisitive about everything he sees out of the window that he can hardly bear to not investigate. Or you may have a happy, contented cat who loves to stay at home. His wildest idea of adventure is hissing at the neighborhood cats out of the window or chasing a bee that comes into the house by accident. It is up to you to monitor your cat and his behavior and decide if the indoor life is best for him and if he is well adjusted to living indoors.

For many reasons alluded to previously, under most circumstances, indoor living is the only viable option for America's feline pets. Some people could not or would not own a cat if it had to go outside because it is too risky for the cat, too much nuisance for the neighborhood, and even against the law or housing restrictions in many communities. Most Americans enjoy their cats indoors and don't really know what problems they face when exposed to the outdoor world. They realize that the cat is so perfectly built to hunt and has well-developed senses for just this purpose and may wonder how he adapts to indoor living and not putting any of these to use.

To understand this paradox, consider the cat. Is it fair to your beautiful and playful kitten, or better yet a pair of kittens, to turn them out the door to face all the acknowledged risks? If they were able to select, which would they choose: a long and carefree life of ease sitting on laps, playing with the children? A life challenged by innovative toys, thriving on the latest feline cuisine? Or would they opt for a short, injury-ridden life? Would your intelligent furry little buddy opt for relatively few years of freedom with anguish or many comfortable, safe years of companionship with its loved ones?

It is true that outside cats are the rule in Great Britain, and indeed much of Europe, but that doesn't mean that the outdoor lifestyle for cats is best for the whole world. Primal, hereditary urges alone don't rule cats' lives. Remember the premise stated earlier in this book: domestic cats have overcome some of their wild progenitors' instincts through selective breeding in domestication. American cats have adapted to indoor lives gradually, increasingly, over hundreds of generations. Let's face it, cat fancy in Great Britain differs from that in America and it will never be the same on both continents. Through selective breeding of both purebred and mixed breeds, American cats usually are quite content and happy to assume the easy indoor life.

LETTING YOUR KITTEN OUT

If you decide to let your kitten go out into its securely fenced backyard, prepare well ahead for its safety. Stay outside with your pet and watch him for indications that he is about to challenge the fence. Train your kitten to walk on a harness and leash. Some cats enjoy brief periods of being on a leash because they know that those times allow it to explore the magic feeling of grass, the sounds of birds in the trees, tree bark to scratch, and all the mystic scents of the outdoors. If you let him go outside, train him to come when called and combine your calling with the sound of shaking of a packet of treats. Withhold his food for a couple of hours before he goes out and leave him out for a very short time, then call him in for a meal. Be sure to establish routine times for backyard excursions and repeat them on a regular schedule. If you begin that process, you should prepare to be badgered each time the cat perceives it's time to go out.

Until they have received their vaccinations and are in excellent health – as early as three months of age – kittens should not be allowed to venture outdoors, even for a brief period. Never let your kitten out of your sight because those little scamps can get themselves into all sorts of trouble with their curiosity and they don't have the experience or sense to get themselves out of trouble.

It is wise to always keep your kitten indoors after dusk when outdoor dangers are greatest and the agile kitten can quickly disappear from your sight. Feed its last meal in the evening on a regular schedule. Cats know and appreciate rigid routines because knowing what is happening next means they don't have to worry about it. They also have very good internal clocks and will be waiting by their plates! This is a rule worth putting into action from kittenhood on so that suppertime means food, safety, and a nice warm cuddly evening with you.

10

Staying Healthy

When you first get your kitten, it is worth checking it all over or even taking it to your veterinarian for a checkup. In this way you can tackle any problems – or, if it is something serious and you have bought the kitten through a breeder, you can take it back if you wish. Even a basic checkup can give you a good idea of the kitten's health. Look at the coat – it should be clean and glossy and the skin smooth and clear underneath. There should be no parasites such as fleas or lice in the coat. Obviously, problems such as fleas can be simply and easily dealt with and should not cause great concern. The kitten's eyes should be bright and clean with no discharge, and the third eyelid (this looks like a thin film of skin across the inner corner of the eye) should not be visible. Presence of the third eyelid sometimes indicates that the kitten is not entirely well. Ears should be clean, and there should be no discharge or wax. Gently open the kitten's mouth by placing your hand over its head and holding it firmly and gently between your thumb and first finger. Then pull down gently on the jaw from the front with your other hand. This does not require great strength but gentle control. It helps if you position the kitten on a table against your front so it cannot back away. The small milk teeth should be clean and white and the gums an even, healthy pale pink. The kitten's breath should not smell.

In addition to being a good quick check, this inspection helps teach the kitten to accept handling and learn that no harm will come to it. Getting the kitten to let you look in its mouth and ears at this stage may be very useful when you have a problem with it as a fully grown cat. If you are at all worried about anything you find, take your kitten to the veterinarian.

That brings us to actually finding a good cat veterinarian. If you are fortunate enough to live somewhere where there is a cat-only veterinary practice, you are very lucky. There are a few around the country, and they are becoming more common. Some other practices may use their branch offices for feline-only services, and still others have times when only cats come in. As a cat owner you can imagine how lovely it is to sit in the veterinary waiting room and not have to worry about your cat getting upset because there are strange dogs close by. However, most of us still have to use a practice that deals with all types of animals and a waiting room that has a mixture of all sorts. Look for a facility, with a high standard of care and a caring and knowledgeable staff. You can take it a step further by asking if there is a veterinarian there with a genuine interest in cats – quite often there will be someone who likes treating cats more than dogs or other pets and, although they may not do so exclusively, you will be able to tell that they have a genuine interest in, and empathy for, the animals. Once you have found your ideal feline veterinarian, stick to him or her like glue!

A separate waiting area for cats, or a time when there will only be cats in the waiting room, will give a good indication that the practice is feline-friendly. Ask if the practice or any of the veterinarians are members of the American Association of Feline Practitioners – this again is a good indication there is a strong interest in cats there and that the practice is receiving all the literature about advances in feline medicine.

You also have the option of asking for a second opinion if you feel that you want more specialist treatment for your cat. Your own veterinarian may suggest a referral if he or she feels that the staff has come to the end of what they can do in the way of treatment and diagnosis or because they do not have the special facilities that may be required for certain problems. This is something you should do in cooperation with the practice for a specific problem and most veterinarians are very happy to refer to a specialist at another practice or one of the veterinary schools. You might find a feline clinic that has veterinarians who specialize in feline medicine. You can try contacting the American Veterinary Medical Association and the American Animal Hospital Association for additional information on how to locate a feline specialist in your area.

PREVENTIVE CARE FOR YOUR KITTEN

Hopefully when you get your new kitten it will be very healthy and you will not need to visit the veterinarian for any treatments for illness. However, there are various things you need to think about in terms of preventive treatment – vaccination, worm and flea treatments, neutering, and perhaps identification. Let's take these one at a time.

Vaccination

Sometimes we can get a little complacent about vaccination because we do not see many cats coming down with diseases the way we used to in years past. However, there is a lot to consider and you might be forgiven for worrying about vaccinating your cat or thinking that it might not be necessary. There are still very serious arguments for vaccinating cats, though. Vaccination has played a vital role in reducing the prevalence and severity of some feline diseases that can be fatal and there are still plenty of diseases that will affect unprotected cats. However, we are also moving forward in our knowledge of some of the problems of vaccination, such as adverse reactions, and these must all be looked at in proportion – look at the risks and make sensible decisions for your individual cat or kitten.

Vaccinations work by introducing substances to the body that encourage the immune system to respond against the organism responsible for the disease, should it come along. If a vaccinated cat then meets the organism, the immune system's response will protect it against infection and/or development of disease. Vaccines may contain the whole organism (virus, bacterium) or only certain proteins from the organism that are thought to be responsible for producing a protective immune response.

Vaccines may be either "killed" (containing no living organism) or can be "modified live" (containing a live form of the organism that has been rendered incapable of causing disease). All vaccines must be licensed, and they are rigorously tested for quality, safety, and efficacy before they can be used in cats. Below are some of the diseases that we can vaccinate against – other vaccines are also available.

Feline enteritis

I remember very vividly having cats as a child that developed severe diarrhea and died, and, being so upset as the infection spread through a litter of kittens. Feline enteritis – also known as feline panleukopenia and feline parvovirus – is a disease caused by infection with feline parvovirus that causes severe vomiting and diarrhea. The virus is very resistant and can survive for long periods in the environment.

Vaccination against feline infectious enteritis has been extremely successful, and luckily we do not see many cases these days.

Cat flu

Two viruses – feline herpesvirus (FHV-1) and feline calicivirus (FCV) – are responsible for what we call cat "flu." In veterinary terms, this is described as acute upper respiratory tract disease. These two viruses are very, very common, and infection results in a variety of symptoms including sneezing, discharge from the nose and eyes, conjunctivitis, ulcers in the mouth, an inflamed throat, coughing, and, occasionally, pneumonia. Cats can suffer mildly, or the disease can be very severe and occasionally fatal. It can take cats a long time to recover, and there can be lasting damage to the nose or eyes. Many cats also carry the viruses even though they may no longer show any signs of disease, acting as a source of infection for others. Cats catch the flu through close contact among themselves (being sneezed on, interacting during grooming, etc.) or via the hands of people who have touched an infected cat or objects that have been used by infected cats.

Vaccination against FCV and FHV-1 plays a major role in protecting cats from disease and reducing the severity of disease in cats. True, vaccination does not necessarily prevent infection with these viruses (partly because there are many different strains of FCV), but it will protect many cats and reduce the severity of the disease in most others.

Feline chlamydophilosis

This long and virtually unpronounceable name is caused by a bacteria called *Chlamydophila felis* (formerly known as feline *Chlamydia psittaci* and usually just shortened to *chlamydia*). Infection is most common in kittens and young cats from households with lots of cats. Infection results in conjunctivitis – inflammation of the lining of the eye and a discharge from the eyes. Cats may also sneeze a bit or have a runny nose. Vaccination provides protection against the disease, but, like flu vaccination, it does not necessarily prevent infection with the organism. Disease can occur in a vaccinated cat, but in a much milder form.

Feline leukemia

Some cats infected with feline leukemia virus (FeLV) will be able to fight off the virus; others become "persistently infected." Cats that remain infected with the virus generally develop a fatal disease. Most will die or have to be put to sleep within three years of being diagnosed with the infection. The virus attacks the immune system, and the cat may be susceptible to other infections or develop anemia, tumors, or leukemia. Cats pass on the virus by direct contact, usually via the saliva, during activities such as grooming and sharing food bowls over a period of time.

There are now FeLV vaccines that can be used to protect cats. Vaccination may not protect all cats but it will add great protection for most.

Feline bordetellosis

Cats can be infected with the bacterium *Bordetella bronchiseptica*. It may be familiar to you because it also causes "kennel cough" in dogs. In cats, infection with *Bordetella* most often causes signs of upper respiratory tract infection (sneezing and nasal discharge). It is more common in households with lots of cats and can actually spread between dogs and cats. Infections can be treated with antibiotics and are not life threatening for most cats.

When should I vaccinate my kitten?

All the vaccines currently licensed for use are given by injection – either under the skin or into the muscle – with the exception of the *Bordetella* vaccine, which is given as drops in the nose (and requires only a single dose). Kittens are generally given their first vaccination at about nine weeks old and a second dose three to four weeks later to ensure a good immune response. The two doses also help overcome the problems of maternal antibodies, which kittens receive from colostrum (the milk that the mother produces soon after birth). These antibodies help protect the kittens against infection until their immune system is more mature, usually until the kitten is six to ten weeks old. High levels of these maternal antibodies interfere with the vaccine's ability to stimulate a proper immune response from the kitten. A booster vaccination given one year later may enhance the initial vaccine response, especially when immunization might have been less than optimal due to maternal antibodies. Following the initial vaccine course, booster vaccinations (single injections) given at regular intervals will maintain a good level of protection.

Are there any problems associated with vaccination?

Occasionally, and really only quite rarely, cats can have what is called an adverse reaction to a vaccine, or a vaccine can fail to work. The kitten may be under the weather for a few days or may have a small lump where the injection was given, but this usually disappears after a week or two. Such problems are rare and seldom serious, and the benefits of vaccination far outweigh the small risk of an adverse reaction occurring. However, adverse reactions at times can be severe and are therefore a cause for some concern. If you are at all worried that your kitten may be experiencing a bad reaction, be sure to call your veterinarian. Although adverse reactions are typically uncommon, and usually mild and self-limiting in nature, it's best to seek professional advice. One rare but serious adverse reaction is vaccine-site or injection-site sarcoma (tumor), and it is thought to occur with a frequency of approximately 1 per 10,000 doses of vaccine administered. If your kitten develops a lump at the injection site that does not go away after a few weeks, it is always worth checking the problem out with your veterinarian.

Should my kitten be given all the vaccines?

When you go to have your kitten vaccinated, talk to your veterinarian about your kitten's present and expected lifestyle. Depending on the kitten's lifestyle and environment, it may not be at risk of exposure to certain diseases. For example, a cat that is kept strictly indoors in a single-cat household has no appreciable risk of exposure to *Chlamydophila felis* or FeLV infection, which needs direct contact between cats for the organisms to spread. Experts now suggest that you vaccinate all cats against feline enteritis, feline herpesvirus-1, and feline calicivirus. If you intend to let your kitten go outside, seriously consider vaccination against FeLV infection. Talk to your veterinarian about which vaccines your kitten needs. Remember, the risks of not vaccinating your cat far outweigh the risks of doing so.

WORMING YOUR KITTEN

The most common worms that cats get are roundworms and tapeworms. Both of these worms live in the cat's intestines. Even though your kitten may not show any signs of having worms, it is quite likely to be harboring a few roundworms! You may think that your kitten has not been outside or anywhere where it can pick up worms – however, the roundworm called *Toxocara cati* can be passed from the mother cat to her kittens via her milk. Whenever a queen is infected with roundworm, some immature forms of the roundworm (larvae) remain dormant in certain tissues in the body. This causes no harm to the queen, but when she gives birth the larvae move to the mammary glands and to the kittens in the milk. Kittens are less likely to be infected with tapeworms, which are usually picked up by cats eating prey, although one type can be transmitted when a cat swallows an infected flea during grooming.

Because roundworms are very prevalent in kittens, it is important to worm them frequently when they are young. The recommendation is to treat every two weeks from about six weeks of age to sixteen weeks of age, with a drug active against roundworms. Tapeworms are usually only a problem in older cats, so adult cats need to be treated with a drug active against both roundworms and tapeworms. Treatment is recommended every two to six months in adult cats.

There are many different worming products available on the market, which can be obtained from supermarkets and pet shops as well as veterinary offices. Some of these are not as effective as others, so ask your veterinarian about the best preparation to use. Some are also easier to give and some are more palatable to cats – ask which is the easiest, too!

TREATING YOUR KITTEN FOR FLEAS

The most common flea found on cats and dogs is the cat flea. Occasionally, rabbit and hedgehog fleas may be found on cats. New treatments now available for cats mean that fleas can be treated very effectively, easily, and safely.

If you don't know whether your kitten has fleas, you can check by placing it on a sheet of white paper and combing it carefully. A fine-toothed flea comb may trap one or two fleas in the brushings. You may also brush out "flea dirt," which is actually flea feces consisting of undigested cat blood and which looks like a black speck. If you put this on a damp cotton ball, it will slowly dissolve and produce red streaks (blood!).

Fleas are very clever little creatures – what you will find on your kitten are adult fleas. These can produce about fifty eggs a day. The eggs fall off the cat's coat together with flea dirt, which provides food for the hatching larvae. Eggs and larvae will be found anywhere the cat has been, but most often in places where the cat sleeps or where it regularly jumps down (the jolt on landing helps the eggs and dirt fall from the coat). The larvae don't like light and dive into carpets or furniture and turn into cocoons. Once they come out of the cocoon they wait for a passing host – a cat or dog or person. They can wait in the carpet for two years if necessary, but usually the whole cycle takes about fifteen days. Centrally heated homes with wall-to-wall carpets provide ideal conditions for fleas all year round.

If you have not previously had any animals, take your new kitten immediately to get preventive treatment from your veterinarian – you could avoid a carpet full of fleas! If you already have pets with fleas, you may need to treat fleas on the animals and in the house.

A wide range of products is available to kill adult fleas on the cat. The most effective ones are currently only available from the veterinarian. These vary in their formulation, speed, efficacy, duration of action, ease of use, and cost. There are now a variety of what are called spot-ons, which are exceptionally easy to apply. They involve putting drops on the back of the cat's neck and may provide protection against fleas for a month or so. You will need to check at what age these can be safely used on kittens. Cats are very sensitive to some chemicals and drugs, so always follow instructions carefully – this is especially important as kittens are small and easily overdosed. Never, never use a dog's flea treatment on your kitten or cat – it could be very dangerous.

If you have taken in a kitten that has already had some flea treatment, make sure you know what was used and when so that you do not overdose. Tell your veterinarian about any treatments the kitten has had, as they may affect what he or she suggests you use. Flea treatments may also affect other medication or sedation or anesthesia of your kitten if it is required.

If you need to tackle the house as well as the cat, again talk to your veterinarian about immediate treatment and ways to prevent reinfestation – there can be a number of approaches to solving the problem.

NEUTERING YOUR KITTEN

Kittens reach sexual maturity from around the age of five to eight months, and are therefore capable of breeding and producing kittens themselves! There is absolutely no truth to the myth that you should let a cat have one litter of kittens. All this does is add to the mountain of kittens that are looking for loving owners every spring. Neutering a cat – castration in the male (removal of the testes) and spaying the female (removal of the ovaries and uterus) – not only prevents unwanted pregnancies, but it prevents many undesirable behaviors that occur in intact animals. Neutering also greatly reduces fighting and wandering and thus the spread of diseases and the likelihood of cats being run over or coming into danger.

If she is not spayed, a female cat will come into season or "call." This will happen every two to three weeks during the period from January until the autumn if she does not become pregnant. Calling, as its name implies, can be a very noisy affair! Certain drugs can be used to suppress the sexual cycle, but these carry quite a risk of significant side effects in cats and are not recommended for long-term use. So if you are not going to breed from your female kitten, having her spayed will prevent sexual behavior, the risk of kittens, and the risk of diseases associated with the reproductive tract later in life.

When a kitten is spayed, it is given a general anesthetic and the ovaries and uterus are removed through a small cut on the midline of the abdomen. The fur at the site of the incision will have to be shaved before surgery, and your veterinarian will ask you to withhold food beginning the evening before. Usually your kitten will be able to return home the same day, and the skin stitches are generally removed seven to ten days later.

Castration of male kittens involves anesthetizing them and removing both testes through small incisions in the scrotum. As with the spay operation, withholding food beginning the previous evening will be required to minimize potential anesthetic complications, and the kitten can usually go home the same day. The cut required for a castration is normally so small that stitches are not required and kittens recover very quickly indeed.

A cat can be neutered at virtually any age, although it is usually done at four to six months old. Undesirable behavior patterns may be more difficult to alter if cats are neutered when they are older. Some veterinarians will undertake neutering in much younger kittens (two to three months old), which appears to have no adverse effects.

Try to keep your kitten fairly quiet for a day or two after neutering to allow the internal wounds some time to heal. Sometimes kittens are still very eager to jump around, so a kitten pen is ideal to keep the kitten confined for a day or two. If your kitten seems unusually quiet or you feel something is not right, contact your veterinarian to check up on it. If your female kitten starts to lick or bite the stitches and threatens to remove them, ask your veterinarian for a dressing or special collar to prevent it getting at the wound.

If you have a female Siamese cat, you may notice that the hair that grows back over the shaved patch is darker than the rest of the coat. This is because the temperature of the skin there is lower than where it is covered with hair (the same occurs at the points or extremities of the cat, such as the legs, tail, and face, giving the Siamese its characteristic coat pattern). This is only temporary, and as further hair growth occurs, the dark hairs are replaced by normal lighter-colored hairs.

11

Play and Pleasure

Think of a kitten and you think of play, skittishness (funny how this word has "kittish" in the middle!), delight, and fun. No matter how bad our mood, we cannot fail to smile at a kitten at play. Perhaps watching kittens play is so wonderful because they give themselves up to it so completely. The thing they are pursuing is the only thing they see; their reactions are so fast, so intent and directed. They give it everything they have and we marvel at such abandonment – adults seldom have a chance to give themselves up totally to one thing without worry about the consequences, what else they should be doing, the danger they may be in, or the damage they may cause. And strangely enough, while we delight in watching, kittens are deadly serious in their intent.

Of course, puppies play too and are very appealing in their bouncy, enthusiastic way, but their behavior lacks the abandonment of the kitten. Perhaps this is because, like us, dogs are pack animals and the way they behave always has a relevance to their relationships with others. Their instincts always have others at the periphery. Only those who walk alone can have such total focus on themselves and what they are doing.

When I planned this chapter, I wanted to look at play in kittens and why it is so important in their development, especially in the context of hunting and socialization. But play in cats is more than that to us – it is a way in which we define them and is part of the joy of a relationship with a cat. Cats can be such self-contained creatures – this is part of their appeal for many people – and we crave their attention. We love it when they come to us, when they purr for us, and when they talk to us. How rewarding it is for an owner to be able to tempt a cat or kitten from its self-absorption to immediate and total abandonment by rolling a ball or dangling a piece of string! Then there is an element of danger – the animal is in hunt mode, pupils dilated, excited and intent, all wrapped up in a beautiful fur coat, with large eyes and a grace we can only envy. And of course it is not just in the cat's first year that it can have these moments of abandon – cats can be triggered to play right into their old age, and these moments are all the more wonderful as the cat gets older.

Watching kittens at play can give us great insight into the movements and body language that cats use when they are older. There are also movements and postures that we do not see as they get older, so don't miss them while you have the chance. However, as cats get older everything gets much more subtle, much less extreme, and controlled. Watching kittens is like reading a book with big letters or a program aimed at young children – their movements are exaggerated, their reactions are large, and they have no embarrassment about such overreactions. Think of when you accidentally startle a kitten – it immediately jumps into that arched-back defensive posture with its fur raised, up on its toes and ready for action. The next moment it is swaggering up to you with its tail raised and soliciting attention. You will see all those movements and body postures that are outlined in cat-behavior books – the tail held vertically downward, the sideways crab walk, the flattened ears, the Halloween cat with rounded back and bottlebrush vertical tail. We recognize these body postures, but actually we seldom see them in adult cats unless they are pushed to the extreme. Here they are, so common in our kittens, laid out for us to observe. Kittens, like small children, also seem to enjoy treading that thin line between fear and fun and will put themselves into situations they know will be startling again and again. Like children, they learn to control themselves and the situations they are in by pushing themselves emotionally and physically to see how it feels.

If you have read one of my previous books called *What Cats Want*, you will have come across the chapter "What makes a cat?" It approaches the design of a cat from a constructor's point of view; as you progress, you realize that, although killing merely requires sharp teeth and claws, the process of getting close to and immobilizing prey is exceptionally difficult and requires the sophisticated control of a highly specialized set of senses. The cat is not a brute-strength type of killer that clubs its prey to death – even its killing requires finesse and skill as the canine tooth is forced between the vertebrae at the nape of the small creature's back. A top-of-the-chain predator must develop senses and skills in order to outwit creatures that have evolved to avoid such predation. These include fast movements, acute hearing, and an ability to sense danger and act in milliseconds.

A kitten must learn to use its fantastic ability to hear and pinpoint prey from a great distance; it must also learn to move its amazingly subtle body silently and without attracting attention into a position where it can pounce and catch, producing instant strength and speed from a standing start. It has to learn to use its talents, such as an incredible sense of balance, and to coordinate sight, hearing, and a body that can bend in just about any direction. This all needs to be under the kitten's control to enable it to kill its own food. It may need these talents to survive as early as about four months old – it's like asking a seven-year-old to drive your Ferrari! The kitten also has to practice getting along with other cats, dealing with new situations, and learning just how things work. Play strengthens muscles, develops eye–paw coordination, and provides a way to interact with other cats that is not threatening. Let's have a closer look at how kittens learn to control their talents.

If you were asked to define "play," you might bring together words such as "spontaneous," "active," or "energetic" – it is easy to recognize when you see it, but quite hard to define on paper. Those who study this sort of thing have tried to categorize different types of play as a way of looking at the various ways in which kittens behave. They have separated play into "social play," "object play," "locomotory play," and "predatory behavior and play." They have also divided play into "appropriate play" and "play aggression."

Play with another kitten or cat is known as social play (strangely enough!) and begins as early as four weeks old. Initially it develops as chase games, batting with paws, some arching of the back, and some gentle play biting. After a couple of weeks the kitten learns to hide as it creeps up on another kitten, developing a feeling for how its actions impact others without actually making contact. This type of play reaches a peak between nine and fourteen weeks old and then it actually becomes less frequent. Interestingly, at about fourteen weeks play can develop into much rougher play and even into fighting. If kittens are still together between the ages of six and ten months, play can get quite rough and spill over into aggression. In free-living cats such as ferals, this can be the start of the litter splitting up. This can also be a time when human owners bear the brunt of this change in behavior if the kitten has no others to take it out on. Owners can be targets as kittens sneak up, bite, and run, often grabbing ankles. This is another benefit of getting two kittens! Not all kittens do this but when it happens, owners need to redirect the energy and intent to other targets, such as toys.

Of course, kittens also love playing with all sorts of things, such as balls, bits of paper, their mother's tail, and anything they find, especially if it moves on its own or with a little help from them. They also enjoy climbing all over everything and jumping off – just like children. Scientists call this "object play" and it develops later than social play, at about seven or eight weeks old when kittens have developed more eye–paw coordination. By this time they are well on the way to being weaned (if they are not already weaned) and are becoming more independent. As social play decreases at about sixteen weeks old, object play increases, as does investigation of their world – sniffing, climbing, listening, looking, and generally exploring where they are.

From about five weeks old, kittens also start to learn the lessons they will need for hunting – it is termed "predatory behavior." Indeed, if kittens are weaned earlier than normal, it has been found that they start such play earlier and do it more frequently – obviously because nature is preparing them to look after themselves at an earlier age. Kittens begin to learn the sequences of behavior they will need to hunt – this is known as the "eye-stalk-chase-pounce-bite" sequence and is pretty self-explanatory. In a world without humans providing food, a cat would have to catch about ten small animals or birds a day – each of these actual catches requires perhaps ten or more attempts before the object of prey is caught. Thus a cat is occupied and thinking about hunting for 100 to 150 short episodes per day. While some may finish in a couple of seconds, as the bird flies off or the mammal escapes, others will take much more time and energy – usually short bursts of intense energy. You can understand why kittens have bursts of very intensive play and then need to sleep for long periods.

Just because we feed our cats, and thus they do not need to hunt to survive, does not mean that they do not feel the need. Hunger and hunting activities are controlled in different parts of the brain, so, while a cat with plenty of food might not be so motivated to hunt, it will still be stimulated to go into hunt mode by the right triggers – movements or high-pitched noises similar to those produced by small mammals. Cat owners need to give them the opportunity to act out the hunting sequence – the eye-stalk-chase-pounce-bite sequence. While we think of this as play, it is actually more serious for cats and should also make us consider how we actually play with them. Some people use laser pointer-type toys to move a dot of light around for the kitten to follow. This does allow for the eye-stalk-chase-pounce part of the sequence, but is rather disappointing with regard to the actual catch-and-bite part. Therefore, think about games in which the cat actually gets to catch the prey and finish the hunt. Fishing rod-type toys (a toy at the end of a long piece of string that is moved around by the owner holding the rod part) are good because they allow for lots of movement and keep any grabbing and biting away from human hands. Kittens also like toys that make a sound – ones that scratch on the ground or rattle – and are especially attracted to erratic movements similar to those of prey trying to evade capture. Instead of leaving all the toys out all of the time, try rotating them, putting some away and then swapping them so that they remain fresh and interesting. Find out which ones your kitten prefers.

While kittens are small it can be quite funny if they grab hands or ankles in play – it doesn't hurt (much!) and owners usually enjoy the interaction. However, this kind of play can get rather rough as the kitten gets bigger and stronger and its teeth and claws become more serious weapons. Play such as hiding behind the couch and using your fingers as prey by moving them quickly along the top to catch the kitten's attention is fun and we all do it. However, it can get the kitten thinking that human hands are acceptable prey, and as it grows, this spills over into predatory behavior. This can also happen if you use your hands and feet as targets under the covers, making the kitten spring onto them – a great game until the kitten can actually penetrate the layers with teeth or claws and also pounces when you are sleeping.

Sometimes owners, visitors, or even the family dog become prey for kittens as they practice their techniques. Kittens don't make noise when they play attack (this might scare the prey away). Owners are often unwittingly the trigger for the attack, as their movements activate the kitten's natural instincts. Some kittens and cats learn to lie in ambush in certain key places in the house or leap from behind the furniture. It is preferable not to act as your kitten's prey, as it can be painful and frightening, especially for small children. To avoid injury, keep small toys or balls in your pocket or leave them in strategic places so that you can grab and throw them ahead of yourself if you think the cat or kitten is lying in wait. Try not to run, scream, or shove the kitten off, as it may be invigorated by the noise and chase or think that you are joining in the play. It may even react in self-defense. Stay calm and don't react – be as boring as you can while you redirect its energies elsewhere!

Also avoid pushing the kitten too far in play. Sometimes while you are stroking or tickling your kitten, it turns and grabs you with its front paws and rakes your arm with its back legs. Take this as a sign that it is time to stop – the kitten may be overaroused, and this can turn to aggression or at least a defensive action. If our older cats do this, we usually back off quickly and let them be. This sort of behavior is often thought of as the cat being in a state of confusion, and it usually jumps down and grooms – a sign that it needs to calm itself down and relax again. However, because kittens do not really hurt us at this point, we often become macho and keep tickling them, making it into a rough-and-tumble game. The kitten may react in a more and more desperate and aggressive manner because its instincts are telling it to escape. Pushing it into being aggressive on purpose may teach it that it does not have to inhibit its aggression with people. It may even learn to be aggressive in order to avoid the problem again.

If you are going to let your kitten go outdoors when it has reached an appropriate age (around six months), with vaccination and neutering completed, you can be sure that it will get lots of stimulation and exercise out in the big, wide world. If you are considering keeping it inside for all of its life, consider the hunting behaviors outlined above in terms of activity levels required to keep the kitten fit and sane. Energies can spill over onto hunting targets inside the home – passing ankles can be very tempting for the alert young cat looking for an outlet for its natural behaviors. Owners running off or screaming in high-pitched voices add to the excitement and the feeling that this is a chase. Play verges on predation when (unlike play where bites are inhibited and claws are kept sheathed) there is a risk of injury. Another way to help the cat use energy and its natural behaviors is to use a toy that holds dry food and releases pieces as the cat plays with it – these are available in pet shops, or you can make your own by poking holes in a plastic bottle. You can provide much of the cat's daily rations in this way and also hide food around the house so the cat has to look for it rather than just finding it in the bowl. Another way of presenting food is in a woven mat – like a doormat. Hang it up and press nuggets or kibbles into the holes in the weave. Be inventive. Your kitten will need to have the opportunity to investigate new things, go searching, practice hunting behaviors, and keep its mind and body active.

You in Your Kitten's World

Imagine being as small as a kitten and being in a world designed for very tall two-legged creatures who control almost everything you do (or try to) and often ignore all the signals you are putting out about how you feel. It can't be easy. Luckily, if you have been given a good start in life you will be confident enough and inquisitive enough to explore, to interact, and to try to understand what they want of you, while training them at the same time to do what you want.

Think about how your kitten sees the world – it is even quite illuminating to get down to kitten height and see how far away everything is, how feet are large and frightening as they come toward you, and how scary it could be when people swoop down to talk to you or pick you up. However, as a confident kitten, you are already finding out that your little body is actually pretty good at getting you to just about anywhere you want to be. You are light and agile with a great sense of balance; you have crampons on your feet that let you climb just about anything you can get a grip on; you can leap up to several times your own height, jump on passing people, and dash around at high speed when you feel the need. Another bonus (well, it is most of the time) is your curiosity – the old saying does indeed refer to the ability of kittens and cats to stick their noses into all sorts of things that they shouldn't to see what is going on or even to join in. Being nosy helps you to learn as long as it does not get you into too much trouble in the meantime (it is the responsibility of humans to ensure that you don't overdo the curiosity).

I've talked before about the fantastic senses of the cat, but imagine being a teenager knowing you have the agility, the hearing, and the sensitivity of a superhero. As you walk along, your sensitive pads not only cushion against making sounds, but you also can feel vibrations and changes in the ground that give you detailed information about the surface you are walking on – it's probably the same feeling humans have when walking on their hands. Add to this the X-Men factor – a set of razor-sharp claws that can be put into action in an instant for defense, hunting, or climbing. Your eyesight is not brilliant when it comes to color – probably washed-out greens and blues with grays and blacks – but when nighttime comes you can see in what humans regard as almost pitch black. That twilight at dawn and dusk, which most humans find very difficult to see in, is like broad daylight to you. You can creep around in it with no trouble at all, trying out all your superpowers, including one highly sensitive to picking up movement in your environment. If it is getting a bit too dark to see clearly or you are lurking in the gap behind the shed where it is hard to see, switch on the sensitivity forcefield around your head and body. Your whiskers and other special hairs called vibrissae situated over your body (for example, on your elbows) are so sensitive to movement that the slightest brush of a cobweb will alert you to your surroundings and help to guide you through. You can hear sounds at a higher frequency than the lumbering dog, and the fantastic radar dishes on your head can swivel 180 degrees to pinpoint the source of the sound extremely accurately. With these wonderful senses at your disposal, it is no wonder you want to explore and try them all out. Of course, if you do get into danger, your exceptional sense of balance and clever anatomy will allow you to sprint along a thin fence or jump up a huge distance to get away from danger. If worse comes to worst and you do fall off something, you stand a strong chance of landing safely on your feet because your body has turned in the air to face in the right direction even before you have had time to think about it – God was obviously a cat lover when he gave out the talents.

As a cat, you have to learn to hunt in order to survive (unless some nice human takes you in and provides you with everything you need, in which case you only need to do it because you feel like it). But then, you do seem to enjoy the hunt: tracking down your prey, creeping closer, picking the time for the pounce, gathering all of your strength and agility, and letting your senses take over. Then it's time for lots of sleep in a place chosen for safety and comfort.

Considering that cats hunt more by sight, sound, and movement than by scent (though they may source a mousehole or track in this way), the cat has a very good sense of smell and yet another special organ that allows it to concentrate scents and smell/taste them. These senses have more to do with interacting with, or avoiding interaction with, other cats than with hunting.

An adult cat produces scent from glands in its skin; scientists who have profiled these glands have found a great variety of different components. Some are individual to a particular cat, such as its own smell; others are common to all cats and are called pheromones. These pheromones give out a certain message, which cats react to automatically. We don't know when kittens actually begin to produce these scents of their own; it is probably as they approach adolescence, when they will join the adult world of communication about reproduction and other grown-up things! However, kittens probably have the ability to sense these different smells from early on and react to them whether they understand them or not. Cats not only have a visual profile of their world, they have a scent one too. Just how this is set up and maintained can make a great deal of difference in the cat's confidence. While this scent profile may not affect kittens initially, it is something to learn about when thinking about their adult lives and how confident they feel in our homes (see Chapter 13).

As a cat your last sense is taste. It is no surprise to find that, as an obligate carnivore, your taste and smell senses are sensitive to protein and fats in your diet, but not to what humans would term "sweetness." However, as mentioned earlier in this chapter, you have an extra talent when it comes to smells (usually not food smells, but those related to interacting with other cats): you can draw air into a special cigar-shaped tube found in the roof of your mouth through an entrance just behind your front teeth. Here you concentrate smell molecules so that you can smell and taste them – giving you lots more information about what you are investigating. This organ is called the vomeronasal organ, or Jacobson's organ, and is found in other animals such as horses, who draw air into it by raising the top lip (looking to us as if they are laughing). If your owner gives you a catnip toy, you may well draw in the smell in the same way by pulling back your lips and looking as if you are smiling.

As a kitten or cat you are strongly motivated to play and learn to hunt, but you also do all those other things cats love to do. If you look at how a cat spends its day, you will find that it spends about 40 percent of it sleeping (nine or ten hours out of twenty-four); it will rest for 22 percent (about five to six hours); groom for 15 percent (three to four hours); hunt for about 14 percent (three to four hours); and spend 3 percent wandering about and 2 percent feeding. If you are a cat that has to hunt for a living, you may spend as much as 46 percent of your time doing so; the average hunting expedition lasts about 30 minutes and provides aerobic activity as well as a focus for mental activity. Young kittens do need to rest, like young children, but they fill the gaps between naps with highly active play.

Of course, as an agile cat you do have a range of body postures to communicate how you feel. Your highly mobile ears, balancing tail, and highly reactive eyes can all add to the intensity of the message you are trying to get across to another cat, a dog, or a person, depending on the circumstances. In general, when you are relaxed and confident, your hair is flat on your body, your ears are facing forward and alert, your pupils are the size they are in response to the available light (thin slits in bright light, wide open in poor light), your body is held high, and you strut with confidence. If you see someone you like, you are likely to approach with your tail up, rub around them to anoint them with the scent glands that are situated on your face, and then brush the scents around further by following up with a body rub. In this way, individuals are marked as OK and part of the group in which you live. You also take some of their smell onto you – a very clear sign that all is well. You might decide to rub various other parts of the furniture or walls just to make you feel even better (it is the pheromones we discussed earlier that give the feeling of well-being).

If you are threatened, you are likely to flatten your ears and crouch down low to avoid attention. Your eyes will be dilated because of the adrenaline coursing through your body, making it ready to get out of there fast. Your whiskers may be pulled back alongside your cheeks, and your hair is likely to be standing up somewhat and may be pulled up almost vertically if you are frightened further. If you try to sneak away, you may walk sideways to look as if you are larger than you are and scare off your foe, or you may try to slink away. You may give a warning with a hiss and a growl, but only if you are really pushed will you react with violence, scratching, or biting.

As a kitten, you have probably interacted with your humans and used some scent language with them, which they undoubtedly ignored. You may also have tried some body language with them – however, unless it was at the extreme end of the spectrum they are unlikely to have taken too much notice of this, either. They do seem to know that walking up to them with your tail up means you want to interact. You have probably also learned that making an audible sound is what really gets you noticed. As a kitten, you purred as you sucked milk and wailed if you got pushed away from the nest or if you were hungry. This seems to work surprisingly well with humans – they love the purring and encourage it all the time; they try to do something when you meow. You are getting better at directing them to offer food or attention or to open the door – they are not half bad at this! Indeed, it is well worth developing further, being careful to not overuse your power and make them complacent. So you persist with the behaviors that worked when you were a very young kitten – meowing, purring, and kneading. With any luck your human mother will happily take over the nurturing role of your cat mother (who has long since lost interest and thinks you should stand on your own four feet!). Aren't humans wonderful!

13

Growing Up

Earlier in this book we looked at a kitten's stages of development up to what is termed the juvenile phase – it follows the socialization phase from around fourteen weeks old and extends to sexual maturity at around six months old, depending on the breed and time of year. By now the kitten is well developed, its skills are coordinated, and it is able to use its muscles and sense of balance exceptionally well. All of its senses are also fully developed – sight, smell, hearing, taste, and touch. It is able to hunt pretty effectively and perform almost all the behaviors of an adult cat. In free-living circumstances it would be time for kittens to find their own way in life – they would move out of their own volition or their mother may push them to go. In feral groups, the female kittens may stay in the group with their mother but would need to be self-reliant, as their mother may well have another litter to look after. The kitten will continue to learn the full repertoire of adult behavior by dealing with prey and interacting with other cats, especially adult ones.

Kittens grow up remarkably fast: one minute they are babies, the next they can be out all night looking for a mate. What you must remember is that they do reach sexual maturity sometimes before six months old and are capable of bringing more kittens into the world in nine more weeks! Make sure your kitten is neutered from four months onward! Owners who forget can be forgiven for not realizing that their little babies are adults – they are probably still quite small bodily and don't look grown up. Also, realize that, if you have brother and sister kittens, they are not bound by human taboos and morals about sex with relatives, and they will happily produce more kittens together! Your cat won't reach full physical size until it is about a year to eighteen months old. The exact time is difficult to identify and depends on the cat's breed and health. The cat's coat may continue to develop beyond this age, depending on the breed or type.

This is also the time when the vomeronasal organ, which was mentioned in the previous chapter, comes into action. It is yet another one of the cat's exceptional features and provides the cat with a very specialized third chemical sense – a sort of cross between smelling and tasting that allows a cat to sample smells intensely. It is most often used in connection with sexual behavior – you may see your